PRAISE FOR *RAINMAKING MADE SIMPLE*

"Maraia has put together what may be the most practical book available on building a professional practice. His advice is straightforward, readily implementable, and eminently sensible."
David Maister, consultant and author of *Managing the Professional Service Firm, True Professionalism,* and co-author of *The Trusted Advisor*

*"*Rainmaking Made Simple *is a practical primer on the rewards of relationships. Too often, we forget that people want to do business with people they know and trust, not with companies or firms. Taking the time to build relationships is the key to increased business and long-term success. Mark Maraia gives us a commonsense, disciplined approach to sharpening our skills."*
Thomas C. Nelson, President and CEO, National Gypsum Company

"The ideas and methods Mark has set forth in Rainmaking Made Simple *have energized our lawyers with a fresh perspective, not only on marketing but on building relationships with our clients. His approach works."*
Eric D. Daniels, Managing Partner, Robinson & Cole, LLP

*"*Rainmaking Made Simple *is engaging and absolutely on target. It is packed with practical truth about rainmaking. The principles outlined offer an invaluable roadmap to marketing success in the advisory professions. Mark Maraia has blown away the mysteries as to rainmaking. He offers great insights and definitive actions in simple terms. The book blends important practical advice and sound scholarship."*
Mont P. Hoyt, Shook, Hardy & Bacon, LLP

*"*Rainmaking Made Simple *is unquestionably one of the best resources ever produced to assist professionals in developing business. It's a basic survival tool for marketing professional services. You have compiled an easy to read, step-by-step method of developing meaningful relationships with clients."*
Lise Monette, National Marketing Director, McCarthy Tétrault

*"*Rainmaking Made Simple *is a highly relevant and significant contribution to the art of marketing and firm management."*
John E. Tener, Partner, Robinson & Cole, LLP

"I love what I do, but I hate to market it, primarily because I never developed the skill. This book has coached me to make marketing a priority. It has shown me in simple steps how to develop an approach to marketing that is comfortable to me. The process described by Mark Maraia will help me create opportunities to better meet my clients' and potential clients' needs. Improved client service is the focus. Increased business is the inevitable outcome."
Bobbie Wilson, Life and Business Coach, Personal Solutions Institute

"Mark Maraia has written the indispensable guide to selling services. In this comprehensive and practical guidebook, Mark addresses the human issues as well as the skills issues, and gives the professional a clear path through the selling and relationship process. This is an essential addition to any professional's library."
Rick Freedman, author, *The IT Consultant*

"For any service professional who wants to unlock the keys to successful rainmaking, Rainmaking Made Simple: What Every Professional Must Know *is a must read! A consummate coach in business development techniques, Mark guides the reader through every conceivable business situation with a practical step-by-step approach. A terrific reference tool with stand-alone chapters, build your professional services library with this one."*
Susan Tatro Slifer, National Marketing Director,
Kilpatrick Stockton, LLP

*"*Rainmaking Made Simple *is a compilation of Mark's best stuff and a fabulous resource. I will be sharing this volume (which is packed with practical tips) with our accountants and consultants."*
Amy Hoppenrath, Director of Strategic Marketing,
CBIZ Midwest Region

"Mark Maraia, who is known for his dynamic oral presentations, has brought that same excitement to Rainmaking Made Simple. *Mark's coaching is simple, straightforward, and replete with common sense suggestions about generating and retaining clients in a cost-effective and professional manner. Most professionals are uncomfortable with the prospect of approaching potential clients for business. Mark's book is an invaluable tool for a professional seeking to improve his or her rainmaking skills."*
Mike O'Donnell, President, Wheeler, Trigg & Kennedy

"*Mark Maraia set out to provide lawyers and other professionals with a desk book for business development. He has accomplished that goal—and much more. Like his newsletters,* Rainmaking Made Simple *is full of very practical, extremely useful tips and reminders of the (obvious but often forgotten) things we should be doing every day. Pick any chapter and you will quickly find a suggestion that will instantly translate into an action step to expand your practice.*"
Howard L. Bernstein, Partner, Neal, Gerber & Eisneberg

"*Rainmaking Made Simple is a tremendous resource, literally overflowing with proven how-to techniques. I know, because I sought Mark's advice in preparing for a 'beauty contest' to defend one of the most serious cases filed in Virginia in the last decade, and we got the work. I recommend this book to anyone who is interested in creating new relationships and enhancing existing ones, all the while deriving more satisfaction from your professional endeavors.*"
Stephen D. Busch, McGuireWoods, LLP

"*All of us are given and many of us choose to develop unique and valuable skills. Coach Maraia is in the 'development' business with short and simple suggestions for success. He is also in the 'benefits' business because at the end of the day the person being coached, his/her enterprise and society can all benefit.*"
Ron Kessler, Locke Liddell & Sapp, LLP

"*Fast read, sound advice, practical suggestions to grow your business: What more could the busy entrepreneur want? The number of easy-to-implement, money-making ideas Mark has packed into this little book is mind-boggling! I am overwhelmed with the powerful suggestions between these covers!*"
Elaine Biech, author, *The Business of Consulting*

"*This book, written to and for professionals who want to ramp up their marketing effectiveness, is right on the money. From generating referrals to assessing client satisfaction, this book is a must-read for professionals who want to build a practice they can be proud of. Young professionals particularly should read and heed Mr. Maraia's instructions—this book could have been titled, 'The Marketing Habits of Highly Effective Professionals.'*"
Ann Lee Gibson, Ph.D., Legal Marketing Consultant

"Rainmaking Made Simple *takes the mystery out of a process that many professionals ignore because they aren't comfortable selling themselves or their organizations. Mark's common-sense, practical approach to the subject is refreshing. Every aspect of the process is included, along with suggestions for actions to be taken to get the advance and record a success. It should be on everyone's desk as a quick reference!"*
William C. Migneron, Chief Information Officer, Shook, Hardy & Bacon, L.L.P.

"Lawyers should read and then retain this book as an easy and quick reference on how to build client relationships. It contains a wealth of useful tips and reminders which can help all of us in achieving our practice goals. Mark Maraia is a standout in his field, and this book shows why!"
R. Bruce LaBoon, former co-managing partner, Locke, Liddell & Sapp, LLP

"Far more than just added value, this book is amazing in its delivery of crucially important rainmaking advice that should not be overlooked by even the best of rainmakers. Rainmaking Made Simple *is the very best business development partner you can have, aside from the author himself!"*
David I. Matheson, Q.C., McMillan Binch, Toronto

"Mark Maraia gets it. His new book, Rainmaking Made Simple, *gives practical, common-sense advice on how to market professional services based on his years of experience coaching thousands of attorneys, accountants, and other professional service providers. Personal marketing is about personal relationships, and this book helps take the fear out of establishing productive relationships with associates, partners, clients, and potential clients. It is the definitive textbook for anyone who wants to grow his or her professional practice."*
Mark Beese, Director of Marketing, Holland & Hart, LLP

"This book is a masterpiece! Mark has managed to pack much of his knowledge and experience into one volume. Rainmaking Made Simple *has immediate daily application for our accountants. Just today I shared the chapter on networking with a colleague. This is one terrific resource I will use on a daily basis."*
Carol A. Poulson, Market Strategist, RSM McGladrey

"Mark Maraia shares the secrets of his own success at building one of the professional service industry's leading business development coaching practices. A must read, Rainmaking Made Simple *is a one-of-a-kind encyclopedia of practical, ready-to-use tips and tactics for finding, qualifying, pitching, and closing prospects. Short on theory and long on pragmatism, this book is for lawyers and other professionals who want to rise to the top by incorporating sales, marketing, and the highest levels of client service into all of their client interactions. Putting Maraia's tips into action is the closest any professional can come to guaranteeing his or her own success at making rain."*
Peter Zeughauser, Managing Partner, Zeughauser Group and Management Columnist, The American Lawyer

"Mark Maraia has written a book that will make lawyers stop and change their ways. It's a practical, down-to-earth guide on how to get new clients. Mark offers realistic and useable marketing ideas for professionals in every firm setting and sets the readers' priorities straight. It's tremendously useful to any professional who wants to have a steady stream of new business."
Larry Bodine, LawMarketing Portal

*"*Rainmaking Made Simple *is in essence a marketing coach. I think both in-house marketing professionals and practicing lawyers would find it a valuable tool."*
Jennifer Manton, Director of Marketing and Communications, Thelen Reid & Priest, LLP

"Mark's book captures the essence of business development: doing. This 'how to' primer is packed with the information professionals need to be successful in virtually every situation. Beware! After reading it you will have no more excuses for not getting started."
Greg Null, Long Aldridge & Norman

"Mark Maraia presents the keys to the marketing side of law the way no one else does. Clear and concise, he presents useful tools in a compelling and highly readable manner. Make all your young lawyers read it."
Sidney N. (Skip) Herman, Managing Partner, Bartlit Beck Herman Palenchar & Scott

"A great guide, for professionals who want to master the art and skill of marketing their services."
Milton W. Zwicker, B. Comm., LL. of Zwicker Evans Lewis, LLP

PRAISE FOR MARK MARAIA

"I was very highly impressed by Mark Maraia's coaching. The approach he suggested for marketing is great. I particularly loved his idea of tutoring prospective clients. It has changed my attitude about how to deal with people. A client bought $25,000 in training from our firm because I used this technique, and it also helped us land a toxic tort case which may generate as much as $300,000 in fees. My attitude with clients used to be 'If you want to learn about this, pay me.' Now I realize that is not the best approach. Mark has really helped me round out my marketing skills."
John Meyers, Seyfarth, Shaw

"Mark's coaching has been tremendously helpful. I have always considered myself very sales phobic, but Mark has an incredible talent for helping me reframe what I'm doing in order to make the relationship building process feel comfortable and natural. Mark's advice makes sense and plays well in action. I particularly liked his suggestion that I approach every meeting with the mindset of 'what can I do to help?'"
Brenda Feis, Seyfarth, Shaw

"Few professionals providing services to law firms have the insight, skill, and ability to bring about the behavioral change that is often required. Mark Maraia does; he is exceptional. Mark's use of relevant case studies and anecdotes, combined with his extensive coaching experience, enable him to quickly gain and maintain confidence."
Trish Carroll, Minter Ellison

"As an experienced trial lawyer who has attended half a dozen marketing programs, I came into Mark's program with lots of skepticism. Even with the best intentions, I usually forgot everything in a week, no matter how sensible it was in the abstract. Not with Mark's program. The real-world experiences I had during the coaching period helped reinforce how the concepts apply. Most importantly, my behavior has changed!"
Bruce McDermott, Garvey, Schubert & Barer

"Mark's coaching was very helpful and extremely effective. Before working with Mark, I was doing nothing in the marketing arena. The fact that he got me to willingly undertake anything that resembles marketing is a small miracle. The structure Mark laid out for marketing during the firm's retreat was very helpful for people like me where it isn't second-nature, mainly because he made it seem very natural and comfortable. While I have a lot further to go, I think I have made incredible progress in a very short time. Without Mark's diligent support, I would never have gone this far."
Gwen Young, Wheeler Trigg & Kennedy

"Mark has helped me achieve what I previously thought was impossible: have fun while marketing. What I've realized from working with Mark is that relationships and listening are key. Mark's detailed suggestions on specific situations that I face have helped keep me going."
Chris Fenelon, Locke Liddell & Sapp

"It would not be overstating things to say I had an epiphany while working with Mark. I now view networking as putting people together for their mutual benefit. His insights on how to approach my partners for introductions were both practical and useful. I would strongly recommend Mark's services to any lawyer who wants to get better at building client relationships."
Amelia Koch, Locke Liddell & Sapp

"What I liked most about Mark's program was his emphasis not on marketing the firm in a superficial manner, but instead on developing a true legal practice, which means nothing more than being an excellent lawyer who communicates properly with clients and others who need his or her services. Mark helps us to readjust our attitudes and habits to accomplish this difficult task."
Matthew E. Johnson, Sidley & Austin

"I have tried many of Mark's marketing ideas, and they work extremely well. I particularly appreciated Mark's signature suggestion of 'avoid random acts of lunch.' It reflects Mark's fundamental attitude about marketing-know what you are trying to achieve at each encounter with a client or prospect."
Ken Wylie, Sidley & Austin

"I am a big supporter of Mark's talents, both as a participant and as a member of the firm's management committee. I have personally bene-fited from his insights and have seen remarkable changes in some of my partners. For example, after I got a great legal result for one of my clients, Mark showed me a natural way to leverage that result into further introductions within the client organization. Mark's sugges-tions are highly detailed and practical. They work so well that it's hard to believe I wasn't doing some of these things my entire career. If you want to accelerate marketing skills development within your firm, Mark is your man."
Jerry Santangelo, Neal Gerber & Eisenberg

"As a former national board member of the Legal Marketing Associa-tion and after 11 years as marketing director for my firm, I have had an opportunity to hire and observe many trainers in the legal profes-sion and can say Mark Maraia is second to none in delivering value. His unique approach to teaching lawyers involves relentless follow-up (and I do mean relentless!). In short, Mark is terrific at what he does and I would strongly recommend him to any firm that's serious about helping its lawyers to market their skills more effectively."
Linda O'Connell, Robinson & Cole, LLP

"Mark's coaching has had a very positive impact on my marketing efforts. One area Mark really helped me improve is my use of public speaking as a marketing tool. Mark had very good ideas on how to get existing clients involved with the seminar (either through attendance or input into the substance of the seminar) and how to use the semi-nar itself to establish contacts and make advances with potential clients. I heartily recommend him to any firm that wants to get seri-ous about developing marketing skills."
Mike Gamboli, Partridge Snow & Hahn

"I can make an unqualified recommendation of Mark as a marketing coach. As a partner with a considerable book of business, I was not sure what kind of value he might bring to my marketing efforts. He has great insight on what works and how to make the most of oppor-tunities without overdoing it or scaring clients away. I look forward to many more years of working with and learning from him."
Randall Steichen, Dorsey & Whitney, LLP

"As a long-time marketing partner at this firm, I have attended and observed many marketing programs put on for us by numerous consultants. Mark's unique programs focus on individuals and help turn marketing-adverse lawyers into good marketers, and good marketers into excellent ones. Mark delivers value beyond pure marketing; he teaches all of us the arts of entrepreneurship and client focus."
Peter Sipkins, Dorsey & Whitney, LLP

"Mark Maraia is one of the finest outside providers I've ever worked with. In fact, I have urged retaining Mark so that he can be available to the lawyers in our firm on a long-term basis."
George Ferrell, Dorsey & Whitney, LLP

"Mark's program is wonderfully suited for in-house counsel who return to private practice. Mark Maraia proved extremely helpful as I repackaged substantial in-house experiences and insights in order to open a lot of doors with the network of peers who had suddenly become prospective clients. Mark showed me a natural way to do this without being perceived as pushy or intrusive."
Lou Strawn, Locke Liddell & Sapp

"Working with Mark was a fantastic learning experience. He empowered me to use the natural talents I already possessed for rainmaking purposes. Until I met Mark, I was neglecting a vast potential network (more than a thousand people). By utilizing Mark's suggestions, I anticipate many of these people will some day become clients. Mark's ideas and suggestions are practical and work well in the real world."
Greg Piel, Jacobs Chase Frick Kleinkopf & Kelley, LLC

"Your advice is always practical, not theoretical. You give concrete, individualized assistance/coaching that does not require attorneys to drastically change their current practices."
Scott D. Eller, Best & Flanagan LLP

"I thought Mark's coaching was useful and practical, particularly on how to get more out of speaking engagements. Mark's follow-up calls also served as a reminder to keep at marketing, even if I'm incredibly busy."
Jim Matthews, Lindquist & Venum

"As a senior litigation partner in the firm, I personally found Mark's workshops and ideas to be extremely valuable. In one instance, I used Mark's ideas to prepare for and win a beauty contest involving a major piece of litigation that led to seven figures in fees for our firm. With Mark's input, I spent several days preparing for the meeting in order to be fully conversant about the litigation. We planned to give 'something of value' to the prospective client regardless of whether we ultimately were hired. Our team made such a big impression on the client that they hired us as co-counsel for the target defendants rather than the more limited role first contemplated. You won't find a more effective marketing coach for lawyers."
Stephen D. Busch, McGuire Woods, L.L.P.

"Working with Mark has really changed my view of selling. Until I met Mark, I had a total disdain for selling. What I've realized is that selling and marketing in the way Mark suggests is very comfortable and natural. I also know better than to have 'random acts of lunch.' Mark's visit helped me focus on major client relationships instead of getting out there to meet new people."
Don Anderson, McGuire Woods, L.L.P.

"While I am already very effective in the marketing arena, I have learned how to channel my energy in even more productive ways. I would strongly urge the firm to continue this kind of program. I really appreciated Mark's phone calls and the constant encouragement. A pure classroom experience would never have the same impact."
Edward Cerasia II, Proskauer Rose

"Mark's training has been invaluable for my practice and my professional growth. He changed my way of thinking about marketing-from 'getting a client' to 'building a relationship' with people whom I want as clients and friends. Mark's enthusiasm and commitment to his lawyer-clients is impressive and inspiring. I'm glad I know him!"
Linda L. Holstein, Senior Partner, Parsinen Kaplan Rosberg & Gotlieb

"As a senior partner in practice for many years, I was somewhat unsure of the value of having a marketing coach. I was pleasantly surprised by the results. I have nothing but praise for Mark's insights and help."
Norman Kahn, Aird & Berlis

"As the marketing partner of our firm for many years, I thought I had seen every kind of trainer possible until I met Mark Maraia. Mark is more than just an outside provider of services; he becomes an appendage to the firm's marketing efforts. Mark covers basic concepts that for the average lawyer are devilishly hard to apply. Mark's mastery lies in his ability to get lawyers to successfully ACT on the ideas. He has had a transformational effect on their behaviours."
David Matheson, McMillan Binch

"I found Mark's program to be very helpful for three reasons, two which were foreseeable and one which wasn't. First, I needed someone to sketch out the proper structure for a marketing meeting and Mark's program does that extremely well. Second, Mark's friendly follow-up calls kept me on my toes. The real surprise came from learning how to focus on building relationships rather than worry about getting work. The whole approach that Mark advocates has a more comfortable feel to it. I am definitely more effective now than the way I approached it before."
Jim, Partner in the Denver office of an Arizona firm

"The most valuable thing you will get from working with Mark is a different way of thinking about client relationships. Mark got me to expand the boundaries of my thinking beyond anything I'd expected. I am taking more risks, and in one case was successful in asking a long-time client for an introduction to another prospective client. What surprised me was how willing this client was to assist me."
Rick Fay, Hamilton Gaskins Fay & Moon

"Mark Maraia's marketing program was the greatest seminar I've been through since I became an attorney. I am a huge advocate for Mark's practical approach to learning and have recommended to the firm leaders that every lawyer in our firm can benefit from his program. In less than 60 days, I have generated tangible new business from two clients that pays for our investment in Mark's program many times over."
Chris Nesbit, Smith Helms Mulliss & Moore, L.L.P.

"I heartily endorse Mark's program. It does force you to make individual effort. My marketing has gotten more focused because I have a goal in mind before every phone call or meeting."
David Viar, Raymond & Prokop

"Mark's program was great because it crosses the huge chasm between dispensing bromides and offering real, practical application. I am more alert about spotting marketing opportunities now. There is nothing particularly hard about any of this; it's a matter of developing the discipline to do it. Mark was the motivating force I needed to become more disciplined."
David Pickle, Kilpatrick Stockton, LLP

"I found Mark's presentation highly useful because it contained concrete, practical ideas on how to deal with real-world marketing situations. In my experience, training with top-caliber people is where the payoff lies, and for training on legal marketing I think Mark is as good as there is."
Mark Wincek, Kilpatrick Stockton, LLP

"As a former government lawyer, I found Mark's coaching to be a very valuable way to quickly ramp up my marketing skills. Mark provided a multitude of ideas on how to generate interest in a recent talk, and they all worked very well. Mark also offered novel ideas on how to grow my network. I am not very comfortable making initial contact with people in a marketing setting. With Mark's help, I found several ways to do this comfortably. He even offered ideas on how to leverage a great topic idea into more speaking opportunities in front of my target audience. I would give him my highest marks."
David Barger, Kilpatrick Stockton, LLP

"I confess that I am, by nature, skeptical of 'lawyer marketing' techniques, as I have historically believed that they simply reflect common sense. Your seminar, however, proved to be tremendously useful in that it transcends the common sense aspects of marketing oneself and one's business. Since the seminar, I have employed many of the methods you taught, some which are counterintuitive to me, with great success. As a result of the seminar, I will continue my marketing efforts as a regular part of my practice. I will also continue to be grateful to you as I gather new clients and rekindle my business relationships with dormant clients. Thanks again."
Mark Bell, Bloom Murr & Accomazzo, P.C.

"I really dreaded going to this program, but I was surprised and completely engaged! Your coaching has given me new-found energy for marketing. I have discovered that marketing can be fun."
Beth Guest, Waller Lansden Dortch & Davis

"Given my role as managing partner of the Houston office, I really found Mark's consistent follow-up very helpful. It makes me focus on marketing, even though I'm plenty busy with legal and management duties. This program was also an excellent starting point for some of the younger lawyers in our office."
Dick Morgan, Shook Hardy & Bacon L.L.P.

"Mark's program vastly exceeded my expectations. His approach was far less sales oriented than I had expected and it places great emphasis on better listening. The techniques I learned from him were totally inoffensive and quite natural. In less than six weeks of working with Mark, I landed two new clients and got more work from two dormant clients."
Joel Funk, Dwyer Huddleson & Ray, P.C.

Rainmaking
Made Simple

What Every Professional Must Know

by Mark M. Maraia

Professional
Services
Publishing

"Keeping Clients Satisfied" was co-authored by Mark Maraia and Jonathan Larson.

"20 Ideas for Increasing Client Satisfaction" is reprinted from *Law Practice Management,* Vol. 21, No. 5, July/August 1995, a publication of the American Bar Association Section of Law Practice Management.

One of the high-energy questions listed in Chapter 26 ("How would I know if I were talking to someone who would be an ideal client for you?") was inspired by a similar question put forth by Bob Burg, in his book *Endless Referrals.*

In order to represent both genders and many professions (as well as protect the anonymity of actual clients), I have occasionally changed occupation and/or gender in retelling the stories.

ISBN: 0-9724532-0-2

Published by
Professional Services Publishing
6834 S. University Boulevard, #142
Littleton, CO 80122
800-791-1042

DEDICATION

To the Creator of all relationships.

TABLE OF CONTENTS

ACKNOWLEDGMENTS

I am forever grateful for the thousands of clients I've worked with through the years who have shown great openness, curiosity, and courage in cultivating professional relationships. This book would not have been as interesting without their stories and experiences. To try and thank all those who contributed would require several books.

Nevertheless, I do want to single out Steve Seifert for his nearly limitless patience and support in giving the impression I have greater mastery of the written word than I really do. I also want to thank David Maister for his generous devotion of time to helping me perfect the readability of the book.

A final thanks to my editor, Matt Holt, for helping me through the travails of publishing my first book. I'm sure it reads better as a result of his efforts.

A special thanks goes to those (not otherwise mentioned above) who were so generous in providing time to review my initial drafts and providing thoughtful feedback: Lincoln Anderson, Howard Lutz, Greg Tiemeier, Elaine Biech, Sue LaFave, and Bob Burg.

I have read hundreds of books on a variety of topics and have tried to write a book that synthesizes that material. If there are times when I have inadvertently failed to give credit for an idea to its proper creator, I hope you'll forgive me.

Special thanks to Nicola Ruskin for the book cover design, to Rebecca Taff for the copy editing/book layout, and to Mark Mattern for the internal diagrams.

A final thanks to my wife, Robin, and my two adorable children, Jenny and Matthew, for putting up with me while bringing this book into existence. Each is, in his or her own way, a phenomenal teacher. My love always.

INTRODUCTION

Many professionals believe they must act in unseemly ways in order to become rainmakers. I vigorously disagree. If this book proves anything it's that you can remain true to yourself and still be great at selling and marketing. In fact, the truer you remain to your self, the more effective your rainmaking.

The best foundation to a professional's practice is the enduring relationships he's formed during his career. If you're like me, these relationships are also the most rewarding aspect of your work. Indeed, what I loved the most as a practicing lawyer was the relationship side of the business. I've written this book with the hope that it will inspire you to make relationships a top priority in your daily practice.

You should notice several principles that underlie everything in this book. As you read, keep the following in mind:

1. Business relationships are personal.
2. Networking is about helping others, not what others can do to help you.
3. Listen far more than talk.
4. Prepare for every marketing contact (phone calls included) and follow up!
5. What clients need is more important than what you need.

Every professional can cultivate the relationship skills needed to find work he or she loves doing. Many professionals settle for work that is uninspiring in part because they haven't developed the skills needed to achieve that end. Professionals who place the greatest emphasis on relationship skills will dominate the market and have the most fun. By the time you finish reading this book, I hope you discover that marketing is more fun than you dreamed imaginable. Nothing would thrill me more than for you to discover that this marketing stuff can add meaning and enjoyment to your practice.

I see relationship skills and rainmaking skills as interchangeable. This book is as much about relationships as it is about marketing or selling. In fact, my letterhead reads "relationship development coach" not "marketing coach." There is a pleasant side effect to this relationship orientation: the more you focus on relationships, the less your services will be seen as a commodity and the higher fees you will command.

There are other books on marketing for professionals, but there is a dearth of books that provide advice on HOW to do it. This book is "light" on theory and "heavy" on skills because professionals have little tolerance for fluff. Each chapter discusses how to make the most of practical situations that professionals face every day: a sales meeting, working a room, an individual networking meeting, a public speaking engagement, a board meeting, a cross selling conversation with a partner, asking a client for a referral and ultimately how to ask for the business—tastefully.

All of the chapters in the skills section of the book provide an easy-to-follow structure for applying each skill. That does not mean it's formulaic. The structure still allows plenty of room for spontaneity and customization.

The ideas set forth in this book are a synthesis of tens of thousands of coaching meetings and phone calls I've had with professionals all over the world. These conversations have allowed me insight into what works and what does not. Most of these professionals were lawyers, but I've worked with other professionals enough to know the lessons they contain are universally applicable to accountants, consultants, architects, engineers, and investment bankers, to name a few.

Each chapter is intentionally short and designed for situations you might face in your practice. They are best read just before you undertake an activity. If you're speaking to a group, read Chapter 34, "Using Speaking to Win New Clients." If you have a meeting with a prospective client, read Chapter 17, "Avoid Random Acts of Lunch." If you're going to a client retirement party or chamber meeting, review Chapter 26, "Working FOR the Room." If you're going to a conference, study Chapter 32, "Conferencing with a Purpose."

Some of these ideas are going to seem like blinding flashes of the obvious but, as many of my clients will testify, it's only obvious AFTER reading them. They admit that the ideas probably would not have occurred to them previously.

I hope these skills look simple as you read this book. Most of the ideas are a restatement of common sense, but as I've discovered from many years of coaching, common sense isn't very common, and it's even less commonly applied.

It is my hope this book will be a desk reference manual you use frequently and repeatedly during the course of your business day. I won't be satisfied until the pages of this book become worn and dog-eared from frequent use.

Let's get started.

Mark M. Maraia
markmaraia@earthlink.net
www.markmaraia.com
Highlands Ranch, Colorado
September 2002

MARKETING ATTITUDE

Shift your attitude that selling is unseemly and instead think of it as helping people find solutions to their problems.

┌─────┐
│ 1 │
└─────┘

YOUR ATTITUDE IS EVERYTHING

HOW CAN I CHANGE MY ATTITUDE TOWARD MARKETING?

Attitude is a rarely discussed topic in professional service firms, but it can heavily influence your success with client and partner relationships. In marketing, as in life, attitude is everything. Richard Bach[1] wrote, "Argue for your limitations and they're yours." He was making a profound observation about attitude. In other words, if you think marketing stinks, it does. If you view it as fun, it will be. Either way, it's a self-fulfilling belief. The wondrous thing about your attitude is that you can choose what you want it to be. You have the ability to choose your attitude as much as you choose the clothes you wear each day.

You might have all the raw talent and skill in the world, but without the right attitude you'll fail to reach your potential. Too many professionals have chosen to be apathetic, if not antagonistic, toward marketing. Many professionals heartily agree with me when I suggest that the typical professional went to professional school so she could avoid marketing. Yet there is nothing inherently evil or unprofessional about marketing. At its core, it's about forming and maintaining relationships. *That* is sacred.

I have noticed a wide gap between a rainmaker's attitude towards marketing and that of the typical professional. For example, one professional views the suggestion to call an old friend as a clear play for business, while the rainmaker might see it as chance to reconnect with an old friend. The difference between the two is all in your attitude. It's obvious that someone who sees it as "reconnecting" is far more likely to actually make the call.

The professionals I coach frequently undergo a profound attitudinal shift during our work together. No matter how often I see this shift, I am always gratified by the transformation. Here are some of the most common attitude adjustments that take place:

1. "I HATE SELLING" BECOMES "HOW CAN I HELP YOU EVEN IF IT DOESN'T BENEFIT ME?" Many professionals hate selling. If you hate selling, realize that what you hate is your perception of what selling is. Most people, including me, hate selling as you perceive it. So change your perception of what it is. Instead of "selling," try helping someone solve his or her problems. Almost every professional I know likes helping people solve their problems. Do more of that and forget about selling. Great selling has more to do with listening, asking great questions, and offering solutions than it does with knowing the right sales techniques. Telling isn't selling.

2. "I SEE A PROBLEM" BECOMES "WHAT A GREAT OPPORTUNITY!" A lawyer I worked with was lamenting the fact that his East Coast office had nothing in the way of a local intellectual property practice. He saw this as a problem. I saw it as an opportunity. He perked up when I suggested he meet with every great intellectual property lawyer in town who didn't have a competing practice for the purpose of setting up a cross referral network. His mindset shifted 180 degrees. He was far more interested in building his network with that clear purpose in mind.

3. "I HATE NETWORKING" BECOMES "WHO AMONG MY FRIENDS AND CLIENTS CAN I PUT TOGETHER FOR THEIR MUTUAL BENEFIT?" Most professionals think of networking as unseemly and something akin to begging. Once again, those who think that way are only off by 180 degrees. The best rainmakers in any profession make a point of putting people (clients and friends) together for their mutual benefit. I have observed many professionals shift their whole networking mindset after as many as 25 or 30 years of practice nearly overnight when they realized that great networking is about focusing on other people instead of on themselves.

One experienced consultant enjoyed a high-powered social network, but she had gotten almost nowhere with it after more than two decades of practice. She shifted her attitude toward networking after being shown a different way. Now she enjoys doing favors for her friends and their children and considers it an important part of her day. This approach worked incredibly well for her and it has spawned loads of work.

4. "I DON'T LIKE REJECTION" BECOMES "I'M ONE STEP CLOSER TO SUCCESS." It's interesting to compare how differently professionals perceive rejection with how great salespeople view rejection. Many professionals take rejection personally and tend to give up quickly on the prospect. The best salespeople, though, think of rejection as bringing them one step closer to an eventual sale! How can it be that the exact same stimulus can produce such diametrically opposed responses? It's almost entirely because of their attitude. Most rainmakers never "see" rejection. What they see is that they have moved one step closer to success.

Your attitude is heavily influenced by your self-perception. If you think of marketing as hat-in-hand requesting favors (self-focused) you'll hate rejection. If, instead, you think of it as offering favors (focus on others) rejection isn't as personal or painful. When I suggest that clients become sounding boards to their high-level friends, they balk. Many ask what they have to offer to the CEO of a major company in their region or of a Fortune 500 company. My answer is almost always "Plenty!" After 10 more minutes of discussion, they start to believe it themselves. Your attitude can and must be "I have lots to offer. Anyone would benefit from lunch with me."

If you sincerely believe that what you offer to the world is of great value, you will never be more than temporarily put off by people who don't show interest in what you offer.

Many professionals don't naturally start out with a great attitude toward client relationships. Firm leaders make the mistake of thinking a professional's poor attitude toward marketing can't be changed. I disagree. I have found a great attitude to be highly contagious. I have been told by many that my own enthusiasm is infectious. The funny thing is I never try to change someone's mind. The more I allow people to maintain their old attitudes, the less pressure they feel to defend them. What I offer instead is differing perspectives and attitudes that they find more appealing than their old views. This gentler approach usually results in a changed attitude.

If you have a great attitude, share it with others freely. One of the finest gifts you can share is your positive attitude about client relationships. If you aren't so inclined, find someone who is and spend more time with him or her.

Consider the proverbial story about the three stonecutters. If you ask each what he is doing, the first one will say he is just cutting stone. The second cutter will say he is making a building. The third one will say he is building a great cathedral. It's not hard to figure out which one has the best attitude. Which one best describes you?

*Double your listening
and you'll double your sales.*

$$\boxed{2}$$

LISTENING WHOLE-HEARTEDLY

How Can I Understand Client Needs?

This may come as a shock to some, but you can consider yourself a good listener and still have a marginal understanding of someone. A non-professional example is illustrative. I recently spoke to a couple who were facing some marital problems. I asked them to rate themselves on how they were doing at understanding their partners' needs. Both of them scored themselves a 2 on a 10-point scale. This left lots of room for improvement. The husband then volunteered that he'd score his listening much higher than his understanding. I consider them synonymous terms. I'll go one step further: It's hard to trust someone you don't understand, and trust is the foundation of any professional-client relationship.

For clarification purposes, when I use the term "listening," I am referring to the skill of understanding client needs. When you have truly worked to understand the client's needs, you will be trusted. Most professionals have never had two minutes worth of training in listening, that is, in understanding through listening; yet it's the foundational skill of all great professionals. It's the key skill for becoming a top rainmaker.

Sadly, professional schools do little to remedy this short-fall. Since 1996, I have taught a pioneering course on client relationships at the University of Denver College of Law. In this class, an overwhelming proportion of the student's grade is determined by how well he or she demonstrates an understanding of what the client needs. Students quickly learn that it's much harder than it sounds.

If I asked you which of your senses is needed to be a great listener, what would your response be? If you said your ears, you're only partially correct. If you said your eyes and ears, you are getting closer. Why are your eyes needed for listening? To discern the emotional component of someone's message.

The way you discern feeling is by reading body language. Studies show that when communication is unclear, only 7 percent of your message comes from your actual choice of words; 38 percent is voice tone, inflection, and timing.[1]

The rest (55 percent) is determined by your body language and nonverbal communication! Our life experience probably backs this finding. When words conflict with actions, which of these two are you more likely to believe? Someone's actions, naturally. We marvel at people who seem to be able to read minds. All they are doing is carefully reading body language.

These studies have some startling implications. Those who can see us (and the visual signals we give off) have more visual data about our message than we have about ourselves. Another implication: Phone calls only allow 45 percent of the message to shine through. And e-mails allow even less. Countless professionals run into difficulties with a client because they communicate solely by telephone or e-mail. That's why I urge professionals to meet with locally based clients frequently.

To be a great listener and thus to engender trust, you need to engage one more part of your anatomy: your heart. Without the desire to understand another person, you quickly limit your effectiveness. Based on my work with thousands of people, bearing out Stephen Covey's *Seven Habits of Highly Effective People*, this is where many of us get hung up. Most people aren't interested in understanding others, but they have an intense longing to be understood. Most of us are simply "waiting for our turn to speak." If two people do this you'll have a "sequential monologue," not a dialogue.

Professionals often spend more time talking than listening when it should be the other way around. That's because there are some huge barriers to listening. Fortunately, most of them are internal and you can overcome them through increased awareness. The biggest obstacle to listening with the intent to understand is our own desire to be right. Other barriers to understanding another include our own desire to be understood, having no desire to understand another, and waiting for our turn to speak.

Suppose a prospective client tells you his current professionals are "not responsive." Most professionals are not the least bit interested in finding out why and immediately launch into telling the client how responsive they are with their clients. This is a huge mistake and a missed opportunity to gain deeper understanding of what the client is after. A better way to handle this situation is to ask for an example. Each client's answer will be different. Ask a dozen different people for examples and you will get a dozen different answers to that question. The answer provided is a road map to why the client might some day hire you. The deadliest form of ignorance is thinking we already know what someone means by "not responsive."

There are considerable advantages in seeking to understand clients. You will become radically better at marketing, because this kind of listening allows hidden client needs and expectations to surface, it helps you clarify your understanding of client expectations, and it builds trust fast! It also reduces client complaints and makes clients more forgiving when you do fall short on service delivery. Most importantly, it conveys to clients that you care!

Selling is ultimately about persuasion. Ironically, the best listeners are often the easiest to persuade and are the most persuasive. If you want to get your way more often, you would be well-served to start understanding others better. Great listeners and most rainmakers have the ability to make you feel completely understood and recognized. They give you the impression that they have all the time in the world for you, even though they have a schedule that would overwhelm most people.

Listening wholeheartedly takes incredible concentration and a strong desire to understand the other person. This is one skill that can be practiced with a host of different people, including your clients, partners, associates, and staff. Even more importantly, it can radically transform family relationships. Try it today with someone you care about.

Marketing meetings are more fun when you are fully prepared.

3

MAKE MARKETING FUN

CAN MARKETING REALLY BE ANY FUN?

There are plenty of professionals throughout the world who believe that making marketing fun is mission impossible. That may be true for some professionals, but in my experience the number is very small. I've said before that you are unlikely to undertake any activity that you equate with street begging or having a root canal. If you make marketing fun, you'll do it more often. If fun seems impossible, then go for challenging or energizing.

So how do you make it fun? First, make it your primary marketing goal. Shift your mindset from "get work" to "have fun" and see how your behavior changes. The ways to make marketing fun, challenging, or energizing are limited only by your creativity and imagination. Here are several ideas to put you in a festive mood.

FOCUS ON EXISTING CLIENTS

Many professionals will actually enjoy marketing if they are allowed to focus on existing clients rather than pursue new ones. Think of marketing as the building and maintaining of relationships, because that's what it is. I am continually surprised by how few professionals have any detailed knowledge about their clients' businesses. Make it a priority to ask one extra question during your next phone conversation with a client that has nothing to do with the matter at hand.

Questions such as "Which competitor do you fear most?" or "What is the hottest trend in your industry?" can often start very interesting and fun conversations.

DO SOMETHING AUDACIOUS

A rainmaker in a large Toronto firm decided he wanted to spend more time in person with a prospective client he knew was flying in from another city for a scheduled meeting. This rainmaker was himself out of town and was flying back from a third city the same morning as this meeting. So he routed his return trip home through his prospective client's city. He also found out which airline and which seat his prospective client was scheduled to occupy during his flight to Toronto. When this prospective client boarded the plane, he was seated right next to this rainmaker! Needless to say, this made a very favorable impression on the client and the rainmaker increased his time with the client by several hours.

PLAY A GAME

Firm managers around the world often complain to me that the average professional is not tuned in to opportunities right in front of her nose. If that describes your firm, play a game called: Finding Prospective Clients in the Newspaper. At your next practice group meeting or partner meeting, break up into teams of five and provide everyone in the room with the same newspaper or business periodical. See which team can come up with the most marketing opportunities in 10 or 20 minutes. Remind them that the entire newspaper is fair game. For example, the employment section of the typical newspaper is filled with companies bragging about how they've grown from 30 to 300 people. It can be a professional service provider's paradise.

One professional engaged his family in a game. He works in a large firm and had scheduled a meeting with a prospective client who was a senior executive of a specialty food manufacturer. He took his coach's admonition to go into the meeting prepared, and to have fun with the process, so a few days before that meeting he carted his three kids off to the grocery store for a family adventure. He turned the due diligence process into a family outing by asking each child to go on a scavenger hunt looking for every product he or she could find with this company's label on it. The child who found the most products with that label won bragging rights. The kids found two dozen products. He purchased every product and then went home and sampled them. He was impressed with the quality of their products. That gave him plenty to discuss with the prospective client, including ideas on color schemes and other matters not strictly within the scope of his professional services. This senior executive walked out of the meeting with 20 ideas. Needless to say, this professional earned all the client's business. The two partners who attended the meeting with him were blown away too.

PREPARE TO HAVE FUN

Part of what makes marketing less fun is rejection. You will experience far less rejection by preparing. One of the most frequently reported benefits of preparation is increased spontaneity and fun. Prepare for your next meeting; don't wing it. It's been my experience that professionals have more fun when they have a structure on how to go about it.

PICK THE RIGHT TOOL FOR YOU

If you hate to write, don't rely heavily on writing articles as your primary mode of marketing. If you love public speaking, then make a point of lining up more speaking engagements. For example, a Colorado professional met a doctor during a conference in Snowmass, near Aspen. They started talking about their shared passion for mountain biking. After the conference, this professional invited the doctor out on a mountain bike ride. Today that doctor is one of his clients and a good friend.

Remember, what one person considers fun, another person might consider torture or inappropriate. If you read these stories too critically, you will miss the larger message. These stories are about how individuals derived fun from a marketing activity. You can do the same thing if you make it your goal. Why not give it a try? There is nothing to lose and a lot to gain.

An initial rejection doesn't mean the client will never hire you.
It only means he has no need for your services right now.

4

LEARNING FROM REJECTION

How Can I Avoid Rejections? (Hint: You Can't!)

One of the largest fears circulating in any profession (and the rest of the human race for that matter) is the fear of rejection. We all hate it. It's perfectly natural to hate rejection, but it's not okay to be paralyzed by it. Some solve the problem by doing little or no marketing. I suppose the thinking is "nothing ventured nothing lost." Avoidance, however, is hardly a solution. To put this topic in a humorous perspective, consider this: If you conducted courtship rituals with the same attitude you adopt while marketing, you'd have remained single your entire life.

Given this fear, you'd think that professionals who actually undertake marketing would do everything possible to minimize rejection, but that's not the case. Many professionals reluctantly engage in marketing, but do no meaningful preparation before meetings. Professionals unknowingly increase their chances of rejection when they wing it in marketing meetings. (For more on the three things you should do to prepare, see Chapter 17, "Avoid Random Acts of Lunch.") Showing up unprepared is not only likely to spawn rejection, but it's the ultimate insult to the person you're meeting.

To minimize your chance of rejection, ask yourself this question before every phone call or meeting: Why should this very busy person invest valuable time in talking with me? Don't pick up the phone or head off to the meeting until you can articulate a compelling answer to that question. If you draw a blank, find a partner or friend who can help you.

Professionals too often conclude rejection has happened before it actually has. It's bad enough that we fear rejection, but it's worse when we see rejection where there is none. For example, suppose a prospective client insists on meeting with you on 24 hours' notice. You move mountains to ready yourself for the meeting and it goes very well. Suppose further that during the meeting the prospect says, "I look forward to working with you," and then proceeds to ignore your follow-up phone calls. More than 90 percent of the professionals I work with interpret the lack of response as a rejection. It may be rude and thoughtless, but it is not a rejection. I interpret this scenario in one of two ways: (1) the client is very busy and doesn't have time to return your calls or (2) since he met with you his priorities have shifted and the issue that was urgent took a back seat to four other more urgent matters.

Rejection is an untouchable subject within many firms. That is a big mistake. Take time to discuss it at your next practice group or firm meeting. Here are some questions firm leaders can ask during such meetings: How do you handle rejection? What makes it so hard to recover after rejection? What is the best strategy for preventing rejection?

Those who fear rejection the most have too much of their self-worth tied up in their successes and failures. Any time you experience rejection, it says absolutely nothing about your self-worth. Only one person can diminish your self-worth and that's you!

Failures can be very instructive. Go to the top producers in your firm and ask them whether they consider their successes or their failures to be more instructive. If they answer candidly, I'd bet they learned more from their failures. The belief circulating in many firms (and sometimes perpetuated by the top producers) is that they were born naturally good at marketing and rarely experience rejection. That's a myth. The best rainmakers in the profession have experienced more rejections than the average professional makes attempts.

What the top producers probably do possess is a thicker skin. They don't take rejection personally. I often encourage rainmakers to share some of their failures with others in their firms. Not only are the failures usually more instructive than the successes, but the rainmakers seem more human and provide encouragement to others to get started and not worry about being perfect.

Consider that the insights expressed in this book are derived in large part from failures, both my own and my clients.' At one time or another, I have made every mistake described here and then some. I'd sheepishly add—most of them more than once. I'm a poster child for learning from failure. The value of those experiences is immeasurable if absorbed with a learning attitude.

No matter how thick-skinned you are or how much you prepare, rejection is unavoidable. There are several things you can do to soften the impact:

ADOPT A LEARNING ATTITUDE TOWARD REJECTION

If you experience rejection but never go back to the person who chose not to hire you and find out how she made her choice, you're destined to keep repeating the same errors. Next time someone says, "We chose someone else," don't recoil in horror. Instead, swallow your pride and go one uncomfortable step further: Invite her to lunch to find out how she arrived at this decision. View that meeting or phone call as one of the most prized learning opportunities you'll have that month. Make it your highest priority to find out what you can from the rejection. Think of failure as intense learning with unwanted results.

Work at Developing a Relationship
Rather Than Getting Work

After the prospect says, "No," the pressure's off. Just because the client won't hire you doesn't mean he will never meet with you. Without further meetings or contact, your ability to develop a relationship is severely limited. Successful marketers usually stay in touch with people who initially reject their overtures to meet because they genuinely believe they have something of great value to offer and no amount of rejection dissuades them.

Don't Interpret "No" to Mean "Never"

Rarely are prospects telling you to go away forever. For example, suppose a prospective client says, "We're not interested. We are delighted with our current professionals." Is this a permanent rejection? In most cases, the answer is no. When you hear a comment that sounds like rejection, the client is not rejecting you; rather, he is saying, "I don't have a need for your services *right now*." Suppose the professional currently delighting the client delegates the work to an associate or he retires. You'd better stay in touch or you'll miss an opportunity.

Don't Mistake an Objection for a Rejection

The client who says you're too expensive isn't rejecting you; she's simply raising an objection. Don't fold your tent prematurely.

The bottom line is that many professionals are too sensitive to rejection. I hope you look at rejection in an entirely different way. It is without question a highly underrated form of learning.

Be a rainmaker, not an excuse maker.

$$\boxed{5}$$

EXCUSES FOR FAILING TO MARKET

What Are the Most Common Excuses for Not Marketing?

During the past few years, I have made thousands of follow-up calls to professionals, and I always hear the same predictable excuses for why they are not marketing. It's no secret that professionals would much rather practice their trades than undertake marketing. Yet they have a skewed perception of marketing. Many professionals think of the proverbial stockbroker making cold calls or some other pejorative stereotype. Professionals don't hate marketing; they hate their perception of what marketing is. How does this relate to making excuses? If you think of an activity as tantamount to street begging, you probably won't do much of it. Frequently, the professionals I work with make a dramatic shift in how they think about marketing. By contrast, great performers enjoy the process and rarely make excuses. In fact, it's the predominant difference between the average professional and the best rainmakers. Your firm is likely to have more excuse makers than rainmakers. I have heard just about every possible excuse a professional might offer to throw me off the trail. Here are the three most common ones I hear and how I respond to them.

"I'm Too Busy. The Last Thing I Want Is More Work"

When you hear this, come right back with four questions. First, ask "Is 100 percent of the work you are doing totally fun?" If not, and it never is, suggest that the person become extra choosy about the work that he or she pursues. This allows the person to go after more fun work while he or she has that luxury. Another question that tends to stop a certain number of professionals in their tracks is to ask, "Have you raised your rates lately?"

If these first two questions don't work, focus on delegation skills. Ask, "How much of your work can be delegated?" The answers to this question are often telling. Many admit they should learn to be better delegators, but never actually do it. If so, spend time rehearsing how to delegate the more routine work to an associate. In some hot practice areas such as M&A or intellectual property, there are not enough qualified associates to handle the work. In those cases, there may be no one to delegate to.

The last question you might ask of a professional who claims to be too busy to market is: "Have you thought of firing your worst clients?" Many professionals become giddy at the thought of not having to deal with some of their least profitable clients. Often they say the least profitable ones are the most difficult and demanding. Life is too short; fire them! Some professionals are concerned that their billable hours will dip. If they do, they can use the extra time to go after more desirable clients.

There is another approach you can take with professionals who complain of being too busy. When confronted with "I'm too busy," the marketing director of a large West Coast firm asks professionals a hypothetical question: "If your biggest client handed you another major project, would you take it?" If the answer is yes, then they have time for marketing. Pretty crafty.

Of course, the most obvious solution to this problem is to get the person to bring in work that others can do. Not only can this mean work for your junior people, it can also mean work for partners within a different practice area. For some reason, this solution doesn't penetrate most busy professionals' consciousness. It's the best of all possible worlds. You can still spend time marketing, but it doesn't increase your workload.

Dig behind the "too busy" excuse and you are likely to hear one or both of the next excuses.

"I Don't Like Selling; It's Unprofessional/Unethical. I'm Not the Pushy Sales Type"

It surprises most professionals when I tell them not to sell anything during the period we work together. There are plenty of misconceptions about selling floating around the professions. The notion that selling should happen immediately is clearly a big one. Who said you have to be pushy? The last thing I want anyone reading this to do is push himself or his services on someone who doesn't need help. In some cases, I will enjoin the more timid professionals I coach as follows: Absolutely do not try to sell anything for the next 30 days! This surprises them and takes the pressure off. It also frees them to become more natural in their approach to clients and others. What I do urge professionals to do is become much more attuned to the needs, both personal and corporate, of their prospective clients. This requires them to do more homework and preparation on whomever they have targeted. Some feel this will ruin their spontaneity. They are surprised to learn how spontaneous and natural they feel when they are thoroughly prepared. More often than not, the professionals who initially hated selling report greater enjoyment from their marketing activities when they go into meetings fully prepared.

"The Firm Provides No Incentives for Marketing; All They Want Is Billable Hours"

Maybe so, but that's a cop-out most of the time. What at least half the population means by that statement is, "I really don't like marketing." What's really stopping many professionals from marketing is fear. If that describes you, welcome to the club. That describes all of us. The title of a self-help book is often what I tell professionals: *Feel the Fear and Do It Anyway.*

If they wait for the fear to subside before they undertake marketing, they'll wait forever.

If you're coaching professionals consumed by fear of marketing, get them focused on a course of action that moves them slightly outside their comfort zones. Every person's discomfort level is different, so listen carefully for clues that you pushed them too far. One way to check fear levels is to ask: "Is this too far outside your zone of comfort?" If they say it is, then scale back the action plan. The greater the fear, the smaller the movement they will take. If they say no, give them reassurance that you believe they can do it. And be sure to follow up.

To the other half of the population, it's more a statement about their priorities. Help those who continually neglect marketing to examine their priorities. Frequently, marketing has fallen to the lowest priority task. After becoming consciously aware of this, many professionals move marketing much higher up on their list.

Most of the professionals I work with focus on capturing one client during the period of time we work together. That way I know I'm not overloading them with a heavy time commitment. Yet, there are plenty of times when they still don't make the one phone call they agreed to make. In those instances, I will ask them how much time it would take them to make the call. They realize it's only a few minutes. I sometimes ask them if pursuit of the target client is still a priority. If they say yes, I watch their behavior. If a deadline they set comes and goes several more times, I ask them to help me reconcile their behavior with their words. Don't make the mistake of thinking that you need to tell a professional that he or she must make marketing a high priority. That approach rarely works. It's much more effective to have the person tell you that it's a priority.

How else can you get someone to move it up on the list of priorities? Make the activity fun. Urge professionals to undertake marketing activities that they genuinely enjoy. Those activities may not always yield the best results; but so what? At least they get in motion. Once they are in motion, they develop a sense of momentum. With that comes a willingness to try other ideas that are more likely to bear fruit. If the professionals you are coaching have a huge mental block about selling, then refocus their efforts on the less aggressive activity of networking. Most professionals make the fundamental error of thinking that networking is about what you can get from someone, when it's the exact opposite. Great networkers have the mindset of what they can give to someone else. It's also the mindset of professionals who are having fun networking. The senior partner in one Los Angeles firm put it succinctly, "I used to think of myself as a supplicant. Now I view myself as someone who has lots of valuable advice (both professional and non-professional) to give to people in my network."

Professionals will move marketing higher on their list of priorities if it provides immediate gratification. A young partner in a large firm came up to me during a break in one of my workshops. He said he had helped someone get a job as in-house counsel for one of his clients. He then went on to lament the fact that marketing does not provide for immediate gratification. I asked him if helping his client without expecting anything in return felt good. He agreed that it did. That sounds like instant gratification to me. Do that every day and you'll be a great rainmaker in no time.

As a leader, be alert to the excuses you hear for *not* marketing. Rarely should the excuses tossed at you be accepted at face value. Instead, probe deeper and you'll find the person needs help getting past his or her psychological barriers to marketing.

Use the same calendaring system for your marketing activities as you do for your professional deadlines.

6

INTEGRATING MARKETING INTO YOUR DAILY PRACTICE

HOW DO I INTEGRATE MARKETING INTO MY DAILY PRACTICE?

Most professionals are reactive when it comes to marketing. That's in part due to the nature of many professions, which are often reactive. We respond to client-imposed deadlines or requests. On top of that, most professionals make marketing a low priority. Yet, the more time you invest in marketing now, the less dependent you will be on others later for your work. The key to integrating your marketing is to have some kind of system that works for you. From experience, I've learned that most professionals have no system or have an ineffective one. The best rainmakers in any firm always have some kind of system. There is no single system that is optimal because you all have different practices and comfort levels. What works well for one person will not work at all for another. Keep experimenting until you find something that works for you. Here are some elements of an effective system:

Write Out All Actions in Very Specific Language

Regardless of the system you use, make sure the entries are very specific. Not "Call Bill Hithrop," but "Call Bill Hithrop by October 29th and ask him how implementation of the drug testing program is going." I can't count the number of times professionals have moved up the date they agree to take action once they have articulated a specific action. Write out at least one question you will use to begin the conversation. When you finish the dialogue with your contact, be sure to make a written note of the next question you might ask to follow up six to eight weeks hence.

Avoid Aspirational Entries in Your Reminder System

Make sure that the entries are action items, not aspirational ones. Instead of "Figure out how to meet Ann Meade, CEO of eToy," make your entry "Call Ann Meade's mother, Betty, whom I know from the opera board of directors, within the next two weeks and invite her to lunch the week of November 2nd." It should be obvious which of these two entries is more likely to happen.

Instead of "Offer to speak at the Electroplaters of America Conference," make your entry "Identify the name of the conference chairperson for the Electroplaters of America Conference being held in Chicago in June and offer to speak on new clean air regulations affecting electroplating industry."

Set Aside Some Time at Least Once a Week

This means writing the word "marketing" into your calendar with an arrow blocking off the time and treating it as if it were a meeting with your most valued client. Hold all incoming calls unless it's marketing related.

This time might be used for initiating calls to existing and prospective clients for meetings, calling existing clients to give them a status update, or sharing an article with someone in your network. Visiting a client website can be another productive way to make use of this marketing time.

Some professionals can't set aside a particular day because

their practices are too intense. Project-based professionals, for example, aren't interested in marketing while they are in the midst of the crunch on a big project and during the days or weeks leading up to the crunch. After that, however, is a fertile time to give that Rolodex a workout. I met with one such professional who had just finished a big project. He realized he could use the entire week to catch up with people whom he hadn't talked to in a while. He used his down time after conclusion of his project for marketing activities. As he put it, he has a lot of energy after the successful conclusion of a project and it makes sense to channel it into marketing. The confidence from finishing his projects spills over into his marketing. He feels no great need to bill time, as he is coming off a fantastic revenue month. He can even use his suddenly found time as an excuse when calling people. So if you're such a professional, schedule a marketing day into your calendar immediately after the conclusion of your next project.

STAY HIGH ON THE HIERARCHY OF CONTACTS

The starting point, as well as the raw material for a successful practice, is the relationships you've formed during your lifetime. Given this emphasis, it's important to understand my preferred hierarchy of contacts. Generally speaking, you will cultivate better relationships if you remain higher on the contacts pyramid. Where you have a choice, ALWAYS go for the contacts listed as high on the pyramid on the next page as is humanly possible. Too often, professionals default to the written word (usually e-mail) and miss out on the more interactive forms of contact. Here are my preferred methods for contact in order of preference:

1. MEETINGS. Meetings are the best of all ways to create and strengthen relationships. When professionals have never met a client who lives in another city, I always urge them to go visit! This is born from my experience as a practicing lawyer and my work as a coach. I've found that the more you see clients, the stronger the relationship gets and the greater likelihood of getting more work. The flip side is also true: You are less likely to be fired by clients who have met you.

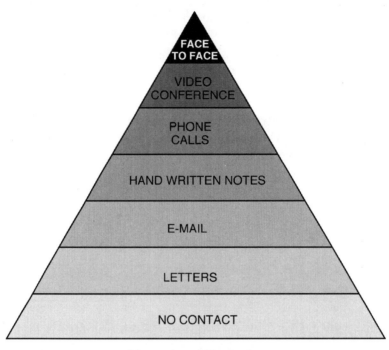

Hierarchy of Contacts

2. VIDEOCONFERENCES. Videoconferencing is an emerging tool that allows for better communication than a simple telephone call, since it adds the visual component of communication. Where your firm has the in-house capability, use it instead of the telephone.

3. PHONE CALLS. Phone calls are next on the hierarchy. They win out over written communications because they allow for interaction with people in real time. You can react to nuances that you can't pick up from the written word. That does not mean your clients prefer speaking with you by phone instead of using e-mail. It means you are far more likely to cultivate lasting relationships via the telephone than you can with written correspondence.

4. HAND-WRITTEN NOTES. Hand-written thank you notes and letters are a very effective relationship building tool. All of us remember vividly the heartfelt thank you notes we've

received during our careers. It's a great personal touch that seems to be a dying practice in this electronic age.

5. E-MAIL MESSAGES. E-mail comes next as a relationship tool, as it allows the receiver to hit the reply key and send back very short responses. It's so dynamic you can almost have a real-time interchange. Some clients would prefer it if you communicated with them solely via e-mail. This is a rare instance where I want you to ignore your client's wishes. This is a sure road to weaker relationships. Malpractice and misunderstandings are almost inevitable. I'm not suggesting you call clients every time and ignore their wishes—only that we tend to use e-mail too often as a convenient "short cut" that ends up contributing to the unraveling of more relationships than you realize.

6. WRITTEN LETTERS. Written letters come next. They are less effective, given the inability for the person receiving one to respond fast and informally. Whereas e-mail allows for one-word answers, you'd never see a one-word answer via letter.

7. NO CONTACT. At the bottom of the hierarchy is a total absence of contact—all too often the "preferred" method for building relationships. Busy professionals end up unintentionally cutting off contact with clients and people in their network. This hiatus from interaction does serious damage to almost any relationship. It allows your competitors to ingratiate themselves with your clients, dormant clients, and referral sources. Don't ever allow this level to become your primary marketing strategy.

WRITE A NOTE ON YOUR CALENDAR TO FOLLOW UP WITH THE PERSON TO SEE WHAT SHE DID WITH YOUR ADVICE

One top-flight consultant I know says she uses Mondays to follow up on advice she has given clients and others during the past week. Another professional makes those calls on Friday. The value of making this practice part of your system can't be overstated. Following up on advice you give isn't just good marketing; it's a fundamental service skill that the best professionals in the world make a staple of their practice.

One professional had given advice to a client on a corporate compliance program. When I asked her if the client implemented her suggestions, she didn't know. She followed up, and at the client's request secured a continuing role at her usual hourly rate in the implementation phase. After that success, she realized there were two other clients who were in a similar situation. She contacted them as well.

Stay Very Focused

Some professionals I know suffer from having too many marketing tasks on their plates. This leads to paralysis. Pick between one and three doable tasks every week. Start with fewer rather than more action items. If you finish those and want to spend more time doing something, you can do so. One professional gave me a list of 67 people he wanted to start making more regular contact with. That's too many people. Instead, make a point of calling just three people from that list each week for the next four months.

Have an Objective for Every Phone Call or Meeting

I suggest you write out your objective, not because you'll forget why you called, but because it will discipline you to be sure you have a clear objective in mind. Before you pick up the phone, be very clear about what you hope to accomplish. If it's an existing client, you can offer to do a tour of his operation or plant. If it's a referral source, perhaps an offer to meet for lunch is your objective. Huge blocks of marketing time are wasted when you fail to follow this step.

Broaden Your Definition of Marketing

Some professionals bog down because of how they define marketing. If you only think of marketing as going after *new* clients and you're overwhelmed with work, you won't do any marketing. If, however, you think of marketing as what you can do for existing clients that delivers greater value, then you are more likely to make the time. Very busy professionals fail to give their existing clients extra attention, and that's bad for business.

For example, one of my clients had been doing a criminal investigation for a large company and had amassed hundreds of hours learning about its operations and the operations of its competitors. Upon reflection, he realized that his client had nothing to show for its large professional bills and concluded it would be a good idea to send his contact a summary setting forth what he'd learned so far, even though the client hadn't yet asked for one. He called his contact and offered this summary. The client warmly embraced the offer and even asked for another summary the professional had not considered. The fact that this professional initiated the idea of doing a summary demonstrated his responsiveness. Perhaps the most striking part of this example is that this professional was initially hesitant to offer to do this summary, given his required workload. His client's strongly favorable reaction, however, became a huge motivating force for him doing it. This is repeated over and over again with the professionals I coach. They are initially reluctant to do something outside their usual routine, but after seeing the client's favorable reaction to their offer they become enthused.

Do Things That You Think Are Fun

If you view marketing as torture, you won't do it. Instead, view this as building relationships with people whom you'd like to spend more time with. For example, one mergers and acquisitions professional realized she never carved out any face-to-face time with her clients in another city. Even though she knew a dozen or more clients in that city, she never made extra time during her visits to meet with them. She resolved to meet with them, called four people, all of whom were thrilled that they could meet her without a current deal hanging over their heads. The value to this professional's sense of enjoyment of her practice was priceless.

Many professionals left to their own devices practice their trades rather than undertake marketing. That's partly a result of years of conditioning and is reinforced by most firms' compensation systems. Remember this: If it took you five, ten, or fifteen years to fall into your current pattern, you are not likely to develop new habits overnight. Be gentle with yourself. One way to break out of your pattern is to find a client you've been wanting to spend more time with or one you want to pursue and put him first on your list of marketing to do's. Then focus on this client or prospective client to the exclusion of all other marketing activities until it's finished.

Just Say "No"

Learn how to say no so you can say yes to more important things. One newly minted partner was very keen on becoming a power broker in his firm, but he realized that in order to do so he'd have to make better use of the time he spent marketing and say no to worker bee projects that would totally consume him. A senior partner in the firm had just asked him to work on a deal that would totally consume his time for the next six weeks. He mapped out a plan for taking on discrete parts of the deal so it wouldn't be all-consuming and thereby freed up more time for his rainmaking activities. This professional was in the habit of working twelve to eighteen hours per day, all in support of other professionals' projects. He realized that if he always did work for others, he'd never become self-sustaining, let alone become a powerbroker.

There are hundreds of different ways to make marketing a more natural and enjoyable part of your everyday practice. Develop a system that works for you and stay with it. You'll enjoy the rewards if you persist.

If you don't know what your priorities are, you can't live in accordance with them.

┌─────┐
│ 7 │
└─────┘

LIVING YOUR PRIORITIES

How Do I Make Marketing a Priority?

It is so easy for a busy person to put off important things. When you do, you aren't living your priorities, you're lipping them. We've all done it.

Best-selling author Stephen Covey uses a demonstration during one of his seminars to show what it takes to make time for the important things in our lives. He stands at the front of the room with an empty pitcher, three baseball-sized rocks, pebbles, and sand. He proceeds to pour the pebbles and sand into the pitcher and asks someone from the audience to come up and fit in the three big rocks. The person struggles mightily, but finds she can't do it since three-fourths of the pitcher is already filled with sand and pebbles. The solution, of course, is obvious: put the big rocks in first. The lesson for all of us is equally obvious. We must schedule those things in our lives that are the most precious first, and work everything else in around them. Exercise, family, and your spiritual life may each be symbolized by a rock. Do you fit them in first? If not, stop kidding yourself. They are not your highest priorities. The saying "What you are speaks so loudly I can't hear what you're saying" applies here. Don't say you value your associates and staff, then act in a way contrary to what you profess. It will do more harm than good. It will make those around you cynical, and they will accuse you of being duplicitous. Act instead in a way that shows you value them.

Here are three ideas that are simple to describe but very difficult to do. Nonetheless, if you decide to do any one of them you will experience rich benefits from doing so.

START AND END YOUR DAY PEACEFULLY

Professionals today are put under enormous stress. The key is to start and end your day with a quiet mind. My life changed in a profound way when I made the conscious choice to make my peace of mind a top priority. I admit that it's easy to get sucked into thinking we aren't valuable unless we eat, sleep, and drink our clients' priorities. If you never disconnect from those pressures, they will wear you down. Vacations are nice but not frequent enough to preserve your mental health.

I've personally found it helpful to start and end my day by meditating. I started this practice more than 15 years ago while I was still a trial lawyer. I admit I had enormous resistance to the idea because there wasn't enough time. Nevertheless, I did so because peace of mind was a huge priority for me. Now I feel out of kilter if I don't start my day that way. The benefits are beyond measure. My daily meditations have a spiritual foundation, but you can be an atheist and still derive enormous benefit from this practice. For example, I've had countless inspired business ideas come to me during these meditations. There is something about slowing down or quieting the mind that allows you to tap into a bottomless reservoir of creativity that you never realized you possessed. If meditation has no appeal, then try nature walks or yoga or read the Bible or some other inspirational literature each morning for 20 minutes. If 20 minutes is too much, start with five minutes. Work your way up to 10 minutes per day after one month. The most difficult part is getting started. Just remember this: Until you start doing it, it's not a priority.

Focus on Incorporating One Priority at a Time

Don't try to change four behaviors all at once. It's like trying to shoot at four targets. You'll end up missing all of them. Pick one priority and act on it within the next 24 hours. If possible, find a partner who will support you in this effort. For example, you're more likely to go running regularly when you have a partner. If you know your partner will be waiting at the end of your driveway each morning at 6 a.m., your odds of doing what you committed to do increase. If you want to spend more time with your kids, make a date with them right now. Go on, pick up the phone NOW. As a coach, I'm always warning people to expect resistance to the new priority. This resistance can take an endless number of forms. Work at removing one item of resistance at a time. For example, one form of resistance I had to my own meditation was how my spouse might react to this practice. Seems petty now, but back then it was a very big obstacle

Get Better at Saying "No"

Learn to say it nicely but firmly. If you must, practice saying no to yourself in the mirror or practice with your spouse. You can't say no as easily to someone or something unless there is a bigger yes burning inside you.[1] Delegate what you can to associates and staff (without overloading their plates), and use the extra time to live your priorities. Sometimes the most important no you can say is to work. If you don't, you'll wake up one day and realize that you've had a successful career, but you'll feel that something is missing. After reading this chapter, I hope that you find the courage to make one change that is important in your life.

SATISFYING YOUR CLIENTS

To keep high levels of client satisfaction, use the "Golden Rule"—treat your clients as you would like to be treated.

$$8$$

KEEPING CLIENTS SATISFIED

HOW DO I KEEP CLIENTS COMING BACK FOR MORE?

In this market it is increasingly crucial to maintain high levels of client satisfaction. Many firms talk about its importance, but few deliver. This is odd, in that it is also one of the best and easiest ways to gain new and repeat business. As professionals, we tend to focus on our work, not taking the time to check on our communication with clients, on their level of satisfaction with our work, and on their overall feelings of confidence in us and our firm's abilities to handle their problems. In this chapter, I will suggest several ways you can improve and enhance client satisfaction.

COMMUNICATE UP FRONT WITH THE CLIENT

Think back to the last file you opened. Did your clients know the answers to the following questions:

- How will I be billed for your services?
- Which professional(s) will work on my file?
- How long is it going to take for you to complete my work?
- What are the possible outcomes of my case?

- How often will I hear from you about my case or file?
- How will I get in touch with you to ask questions?
- How quickly can I expect you to return my calls?
- Who else can I contact if you're not available?
- What control do I have over my case or file?

Did you know the answers to these questions? These issues can and should be addressed up front or trouble is likely to follow.

We all have client fee agreements that we give clients to review and sign. Most of these are designed for our legal protection instead of for the client's information and peace of mind. We can still address the issues we need to in order to protect ourselves, while fully communicating what is important to the client. Try submitting your fee agreements with the above client issues addressed or set them out in a separate document; then review it in person with the client so that these issues are brought out in the beginning. This avoids subsequent misunderstandings and helps the client understand what to expect from you and your firm. Be prepared to deliver what you promise. To set expectations with the client in the beginning, and then not deliver as promised, will cause more harm than not doing it at all.

RETURN CLIENT PHONE CALLS PROMPTLY

The number one complaint of most clients is that their professionals won't return their calls promptly. This is where we as professionals have failed to set proper expectations with our clients. We should tell our clients, up front, how often they are likely to hear from us, how quickly they can expect to receive a call back from us, and what our schedules are like, to help them know what to expect.

You can't always tell from a client message whether it's urgent or not. One of my clients conducted a client interview and found he had lost the opportunity to handle an employment trial because he did not respond quickly enough to the client's message.

It may surprise you to find out that many large corporations, such as Xerox, IBM, and Hewlett-Packard, have done studies which show that the timeliness of return phone calls by their salespeople is directly related to overall sales success. Calls returned within two hours have a 90 percent greater chance of gaining business than those returned even after only 24 hours! When it's a call from a customer, customer satisfaction increases if calls are returned promptly, even when you can't immediately resolve the problem! This at least shows your concern for the client and her problem.

How does this affect professionals? When you are returning phone calls, you need to prioritize which clients you call back first. An existing client who calls would rather get a voice mail message from you, or a two-minute call explaining your busy schedule, than to be ignored or put off until the next day. The best rainmakers, however, make their clients feel as if they have all the time in the world for the clients. If you can't call your client back promptly, have your secretary call on your behalf. There are times when clients are unable to gauge the quality of work that you do for them. They then judge the quality of your work on something they can gauge, your response time.

CHECK ON YOUR CLIENT'S SATISFACTION OFTEN

Many of you may already conduct periodic client satisfaction interviews. It can be done in an official capacity by firm leaders or individually by a single professional. Doing so is a regular practice of most top-tier firms. Sometimes we even use the information gained from these to try and improve how we do business. Other times, the information sits in a file, never to be read. This feedback provides a blueprint on how to deepen the existing client relationship and gives you insight on why future clients will buy from you.

Client satisfaction interviews need to be done frequently. If these interviews aren't done frequently, it may be too late to take corrective action. For example, suppose a client satisfaction interview reveals a problem, such as a phone call that went unreturned five months ago. You have missed a chance to correct the problem closer to its occurrence.

In their constant struggle to achieve high quality and customer satisfaction levels, companies such as Saturn, Lexus, Xerox, IBM, Infinity, and others, have set up a systematic approach to gaining world-class customer satisfaction. What they all have in common is getting consistent and repetitive feedback from their customers, and, most importantly, they take immediate action when a problem is encountered. How many of you contact your clients (or have someone in your office do it) on a regular basis to see how you are doing? More importantly, how many have a system to correct problems on an immediate basis? Why should you do this? Prior to your asking for feedback, your client may have *suspected* you didn't care; but after you ask for feedback and do nothing, he or she will *know* that you don't care.

Companies have found that getting regular feedback and acting on it increases customer satisfaction levels to world-class standards. This in turn creates strong customer loyalty and repeat sales. The companies above know that it takes six times the amount of time and money to gain a new customer as it does to keep an existing one. As professionals, we should be doing the same thing with all of our clients. With today's technology, there is no reason that we can't set up similar processes in our own offices.

There are several questions that I would urge you to get in the habit of asking your clients. The first is: "What can we do to become easier to do business with?" Other powerful questions to ask are: "What do you like about the work we've done so far?" and "Is there anything you'd like us to do differently?" This is a nice way to gather difficult feedback from clients that they might not otherwise give.

Keep in Touch with Clients

Many of you have a monthly or quarterly firm newsletter that goes out to all clients and friends of the firm. This is a good way to stay in touch with former or inactive clients. But how many of you actually make a point of calling clients and former clients on a regular basis just to ask how they're doing or to find out what's new with their business? How many stay on top of your client's industry or marketplace and call them when you notice any new or newsworthy information? Most of you have Lexis/Nexis, Westlaw, or some other service that can track a client or marketplace for you on a regular basis, to alert you to any news without having to do anything other than the initial set-up.

You can also visit your client's plant or place of business without charging. This is a tried-and-true method of getting new files. The best rainmakers in the firms that I work with still do this with great success. Client visits show the client that you're more than just a professional; you're a partner.

Spend an hour or two at client websites. There is likely to be a vast amount of information available that you would not have been aware of otherwise. It's marketing malpractice not to visit a website prior to meeting with a prospective client. It's equally unpardonable to forego visits to existing clients' websites. One professional I work with claimed that a client site did not have enough information to spend more than 10 minutes on. She visited the site in spite of her skepticism and reported back that it was full of useful information.

You'll be surprised by how impressed your clients will be when you show an interest in and knowledge of their business and marketplace over and above their professional issues.

Trust is a professional's most valuable stock in trade.

□ 9

TWENTY IDEAS FOR INCREASING CLIENT SATISFACTION

WHAT CONCRETE IDEAS DO YOU HAVE FOR INCREASING CLIENT SATISFACTION?

The gap between the services our clients expect and what we are delivering is getting wider. Technical skills are not enough to ensure our professional success. In order to close the gap, you and your staff must become more focused on what it takes to satisfy client needs. Here are several ideas that will work to close that gap:

1. RECOMMEND WAYS TO HELP YOUR CLIENTS REDUCE THEIR PROFESSIONAL FEES. This might seem like financial suicide, but it's not. Trust, not time, is a professional's most valuable stock in trade. There is no greater demonstration of trustworthiness to clients than your willingness to tell them how to reduce their professional fees. An exercise you might try with your staff is to ask them how they might handle a particular case if it had a cap on fees that are one half of what you've told the client it will cost. Even though such a restraint is artificial, it will force you to think differently about your files. You will likely uncover ways to deliver greater value to your client.

2. TREAT EVERY MEMBER OF YOUR STAFF EXACTLY THE WAY YOU WANT THEM TO TREAT YOUR BEST CLIENTS. If you treat your employees like dirt, your employees are likely to treat your clients in a similar manner. This is an immutable law of human relationships. Like gravity, this law operates independent of our awareness of it. It's also common sense. Unhappy staff can turn into client satisfaction terrorists. There were many times in my private practice that my clients interacted with my staff (secretary or legal assistant) more frequently than they dealt with me. How is the client likely to perceive my services if his or her experience with my staff was unfavorable? How are your staff's interactions perceived by your clients?

3. CALL YOUR TEN BEST CLIENTS ON A WEEKLY OR PERIODIC BASIS TO DO A STATUS REPORT. I suggest you schedule time on your calendar each month for making these calls. If you just let it happen, it won't. You must place this activity on your calendar for an entire year to ensure that it will be done consistently. This will help create a perception in your client's mind that you are on top of the case. It's not realistic to do this with every client, but it is a surefire client retention strategy with major clients. Don't wait for them to call you or wait for a court-imposed deadline. I know of one managing partner of a three-partner office who did this and it generated multiple new client referrals.

4. MEET WEEKLY WITH ALL EMPLOYEES AND INVITE THEIR FEEDBACK ON WAYS THEY CAN INCREASE CLIENT SATISFACTION. At each meeting, always ask these two questions: "What are we doing of value to client A that he or she may not be aware of?" and "What could we be doing for our client at no cost to us that our client would appreciate enormously?" An example of this might be sending a report to the president of a client company that is in "Board of Directors" ready form at exactly the time needed. This would eliminate the client having to reformat your report. The client is likely to appreciate your removing one of the headaches of his or her job.

5. RECOGNIZE, REWARD, AND PROMOTE PEOPLE BASED ON THEIR ABILITY TO GENERATE SATISFIED CLIENTS. When hiring, how can you gauge a person's client satisfaction skills? Try asking job candidates for several client and co-worker references. If your firm hires those who are technically capable but have a poor "desk-side manner" over those who are service oriented but slightly less brilliant technically, then you're sending the wrong message. Make client satisfaction a significant criteria for promotion to partnership. This can be done by incorporating the results of formal client surveys or peer reviews. It also has implications for your vulnerability to malpractice claims. One 20-lawyer firm that represented hundreds of doctors realized this truth as it relates to doctors they'd defended. In one instance, a brilliant technician had been sued five times, while the less brilliant doctor with an excellent "bedside manner" had botched several operations, but her patients never sued. How can that be? Satisfied clients are more forgiving.

6. CALCULATE THE TEN LARGEST CLIENTS OF THE FIRM AS MEASURED IN TERMS OF LIFETIME VALUE. To do this you must make some assumptions. Look at the trends of each client's billings to see which ones are in a growth mode. Then extrapolate what the firm's revenues might be during the next 10- or 20-year period. An obvious example of a client that didn't have a high lifetime value is the Resolution Trust Corporation (RTC). Since the RTC had a limited statutory existence, it wasn't going to be one of the largest clients five years hence. By contrast, a small software company with $5M in sales and modest professional bills might have a significant lifetime value. Once you've made these calculations, develop specific client retention strategies for the top 10.

7. ROUTINELY SEEK FEEDBACK FROM CLIENTS AFTER EACH COMPLETED TRANSACTION OR ENGAGEMENT. This information is valuable for two reasons. First, it can serve as an early warning system for an existing client's dissatisfaction. And second, the lessons learned from the feedback can be used to understand the needs of prospective clients who are similarly situated. Many professionals are fearful that seeking feedback will "open a can of worms." That may be true, but it is far better to know the painful truth than to enjoy the illusion of comfort. There are many ways to gather that feedback, including written client surveys and peer reviews. One firm of 70 professional service advisors with 30 partners regularly does partner and associate peer reviews. One partner will meet with three to five clients of another professional in order to ascertain the client's level of satisfaction. The results of this feedback can affect their share of the profits. The danger in gathering feedback is that it creates a client expectation that you will act on it. If you aren't prepared to act on the insights gathered, don't seek the feedback.

8. IN ADVANCE OF AN INITIAL CLIENT MEETING, MAIL OR FAX A SET OF QUESTIONS YOUR CLIENT SHOULD BE PREPARED TO ANSWER IN PERSON. If your firm uses checklists, it may be as simple as rewriting the checklist into a question format. Use plain English in the questionnaire and explain all terms that might be misunderstood by a layperson. This accomplishes several things. First, it saves the professional time during the initial meeting, meaning less drudgery in your practice. Second, your client will increase his or her psychological investment in using your firm. Finally, if done properly, the client sees greater value in the services you render without a significant investment of professional time.

9. SET A GOAL OF LEARNING TEN NEW THINGS EACH YEAR ABOUT YOUR FIRM'S BEST CLIENT. You might gather information about the client's specific business goals for the coming year, what its customers want from your client, and its plans for expansion or contraction. It's also helpful to know your client's business mission, vision, goals, and values so you can formulate professional strategies with them in mind. Anything less borders on client satisfaction malpractice.

10. SEND OUT LETTERS OF THANKS/APPRECIATION/GRATITUDE TO ALL CLIENTS UPON COMPLETION OF THE ENGAGEMENT. A simple thank you letter is all that's needed, and you don't even have to do most of the work. Simply design a standard letter and instruct your assistant to prepare it for your signature upon completion of each client matter. You can

always customize the boilerplate letter as the circumstances warrant.

11. WHEN YOUR CLIENT COMPLAINS, FOCUS ON SAVING THE CLIENT, NOT YOUR FEE. Fighting with a client over fees says, "We value payment of our fees over our long-term relationship with you." I'm not suggesting that you just cave in to unreasonable client demands. But you had better consider the lifetime value of the client you're about to irritate. One of my law firm clients was involved in a billing dispute with their client over costs incurred in successful litigation. The amount in dispute was around $10,000 in costs, which the client was contractually obligated to pay. This firm felt that their client's demand that the firm eat these costs was unreasonable. From a contractual standpoint, they were right because the retainer agreement clearly spelled out that the client was obligated to pay costs. I had them consider the lifetime value of this particular client. In such cases, it's wise to save the client, not the fee. When seeing it in that light, the firm's managing partner decided to eat a portion of the disputed costs and saved the client in the process. To date, the firm has received fees from that client on new matters that are six times greater than the costs the firm agreed to absorb.

12. HAVE ALL YOUR PEOPLE KEEP A CLIENT SATISFACTION LOG AND ENTER ALL POSITIVE AND NEGATIVE EXPERIENCES INTO IT. Review both kinds of entries in the log as a team periodically. Recognize your people in some way for making a specified number of entries in this log. It does not matter if you're a firm of three people or three hundred people. This might operate like an "employee of the month" program, except there can be multiple winners! The purpose of this log is threefold. First, it creates employee sensitivity to client satisfaction. Second, it allows the most client-oriented people in your firm to teach the less client-centered employees what great service looks like. Finally, you'll begin to gain a better understanding of what behaviors your employees believe promote client satisfaction. For example, a receptionist's entry might say, "George Smith commented favorably on my ability to recognize his voice before he identified himself." A legal assistant might say, "Client sent a complementary letter about me to my supervising attorney showing my diligence in answering a specific question within one hour of the client's call."

13. SEND BIRTHDAY, HOLIDAY, FOUNDER'S DAY, AND ANNIVERSARY CARDS TO LONGSTANDING CLIENTS. This can be done systematically. For example, if your practice routinely incorporates many businesses each year, have your secretary enter the date the client's articles of incorporation were granted by the secretary of state and put that into a tickler system. Then send out a "birthday" card or letter each year as the anniversary date arises. You can also celebrate longstanding relationships with clients by sending them an anniversary card or letter celebrating the commencement of your professional-client relationship.

14. FOLLOW UP ON EVERY PROPOSAL REJECTED BY A POTENTIAL CLIENT TO LEARN WHAT YOU SHOULD DO DIFFERENTLY NEXT TIME. This is likely to enhance the prospective client's view of your firm. This also allows you to maximize your learning from the "failure." For example, an acknowledged rainmaker (who brought in $3 million annually) of a 40-professional firm in Boston made a solo presentation to a prospective client, but lost out to a competing firm that had made a presentation using four professionals from the firm. This rainmaker, to his credit, went back to the prospective client after learning that the other firm was chosen and asked how he came up short. The client's reply was, "We were looking for a firm that took a team approach to serving our needs; you claimed to have that capacity, but the other firm demonstrated it. We felt you were both technically competent, so it came down to their ability to work as a team in serving us."

15. CONTACT CLIENTS OWING AGING RECEIVABLES AS A MEANS OF GATHERING "MARKET RESEARCH." The assumption here is aging receivables can be evidence of a dissatisfied client. Use the unpaid bill as a pretext for gathering valuable client feedback. This feedback can be used to strengthen your firm's relationship with the slow-paying client, and these same lessons can be applied to other firm clients. It's advisable to

contact the client when the receivable becomes 30 days past due. You must attempt to understand the client's point of view rather than convey your displeasure over nonpayment.

16. RECONFIGURE YOUR PHONE SYSTEM TO PREVENT PUTTING ANY CALLER ON HOLD FOR LONGER THAN 30 SECONDS. Every time a client perceives some aspect of your firm, via telephone or otherwise, he or she forms a conscious or subconscious impression about the quality and value of your firm's services. Your phone system is the equivalent of your firm's front window. We may not think it's a big deal, but consider our thoughts about businesses that send us to electronic "never-never land." These thoughts aren't very favorable. And we're likely to view such businesses as very unconcerned about its clients. In fact, some of the worst offenders are monopolies like the local phone company or cable TV companies.

17. PUT THE FOLLOWING LEGEND ON ALL EMPLOYEE PAYCHECKS: "THIS PAYCHECK WAS MADE POSSIBLE BY A SATISFIED CLIENT." What better way to remind everyone that clients make the world go round. Federal Express, one of the world's best at achieving customer satisfaction, puts this legend on employee paychecks. It's very easy to do, and if it raises the awareness level in one employee it's worth doing.

18. MAKE THE FIRST AGENDA ITEM AT EVERY PARTNER MEETING "CLIENT SATISFACTION." A professional's most valuable commodity is time. Your partners and employees will look at your behavior to determine what you value. If you never discuss client satisfaction at partner meetings, how important can it be? Many firms think they do this, but when pressed they admit that they are merely discussing the technical aspects of a client's case, not their level of satisfaction. How firm leaders invest their meeting time communicates very clearly where their priorities lie. If client satisfaction isn't one of your firm's highest priorities, what is?

19. MAKE A COMPLETE TOUR OF YOUR CLIENT'S PHYSICAL FACILITIES FOR FREE WITH A VIEW TOWARD UNDERSTANDING THE NUANCES OF THEIR BUSINESS. The professionals who make this a regular part of their practice usually deepen their understanding of clients' needs. This in turn generates new business, or at least bullet-proofs the client. Don't try to do this with every client. Instead pick three clients you feel are highly valued and do one per month during the next 90 days.

20. BE AWARE OF THE NONVERBAL SIGNALS YOUR CLIENTS PERCEIVE IN YOUR EVERYDAY BEHAVIOR. Even though many professionals are directly compensated for their ability to persuade and communicate, they unknowingly send out many negative nonverbal messages. Most are completely unaware of the messages they're sending to valued clients. Unfortunately, your clients are not. Everyone is familiar with the old saying "Perception is reality." Well, it's true with clients. Yet many professionals act as if that principle doesn't apply to their client relationships. The attorney who takes off his Rolex watch for a two-week trial in order to cultivate a desired perception with jurors is the same one who'll make his client wait 30 minutes in his firm's reception area. In the 21st Century it won't be the best technical professionals who'll land the best clients. It will be the professionals who are perceived to be the best by their clients and prospective clients.

Here are some common professional behaviors and the corresponding nonverbal messages those behaviors might send to your clients:

1. Sending your statement of professional fees to clients on anything less than high grade paper or using a dot matrix printer communicates this nonverbal message: "This statement isn't very important; take your time for payment." It may also cause the client to wonder if the quality of the professional work you are doing is comparable to the quality of your statement.

2. Making your client wait more than a few minutes in the firm's reception area communicates this nonverbal message: "My time is more valuable and important than your time" or "I'm not very organized and in control."

3. Failure to return a client's phone call promptly (within 24 hours at worst) says, "You're not very important to

me." What's prompt may vary depending on the circumstances, but either you or your assistant should never leave the call unreturned for more than 24 hours, and in some cases that's far too long! Even better is your attempt to reach the client two or more times before he or she attempts to return your call. This action says "You are a very important and valued client."

4. Telling a new client that you've handled "hundreds of cases like this before" may reassure some clients. But to many clients it says, "We take a cookie cutter approach to your problem." The result is clients who perceive that their professional doesn't treat them as unique and special.

5. Allowing your meeting with a client to be interrupted says, "There is some matter in our office that's more important than you." We've all been told to give our clients our undivided attention, and unless you're comfortable sending your client this nonverbal message, you're best to heed this advice.

Don't fool yourself into believing the examples above are isolated and unusual. They are not. When your words and your behavior conflict, people are more likely to believe your actions than your words.

An effective marketing program focuses on keeping your existing clients satisfied. These techniques will enable you to delight even the pickiest clients. Select one or two of the ideas listed and act on them immediately. Good luck!

Invite several clients to your next practice group meeting or part-ner retreat and have them talk about what they like about their service providers and what drives them crazy.

$$\boxed{10}$$

THE CASE FOR GATHERING CLIENT FEEDBACK

I t is the rare firm that makes gathering client feedback a top priority. To test where you stand, answer these questions: Does your firm routinely seek feedback from clients at the end of the engagement? Do individual professionals gather feedback during the course of the engagement? Does your firm gather quantitative feedback from staff on how they are treated by the professionals in your firm? Is everyone in your firm, including partners, paid better when they achieve the highest levels of client and employee satisfaction? Is client sat-isfaction a significant criterion for promotion to partnership? If you answered yes to all, or even most, of these questions, you're way ahead of most firms.

One of the reasons many firms don't make client feedback a top priority is they don't realize the benefits to be gained from this action. In my experience, how professionals think clients perceive them is usually different from how they are actually perceived. If done well, you will end up with more work, you'll learn of problems earlier, and the feedback from one client will often be useful for increasing the loyalty of other clients. Many professionals think they should only be looking for negative feedback. That's clearly not the case. Professionals should be looking not only for negative feedback but also for positive feedback which will help deepen the relationship and understanding of why future clients will buy from you.

Occasionally seeking client feedback doesn't cut it. If you want to put your clients at the center of your business, constant feedback is a must. Leading companies constantly ask for feedback from their customers. They have found through empirical studies that putting customers at the center of their business leads to repeat sales and greater profits.

I urge all my readers to conduct in-person client interviews with your most prized clients. What follows are some objections I've heard from individual professionals and firm leaders to doing so, along with arguments you can use to combat these objections.

A typical partner objection is, "We already know what our clients think about us." It is the height of arrogance for professionals to make this declaration. What are they, clairvoyant? The next time a professional service provider makes that comment, ask for his data for that conclusion. Usually there is none, only speculation and conjecture. The unstated fear is "I'm terrified by what they might say about me." Another common objection is, "Our partners would never allow them." This is probably another way of saying, "I don't want you to do them with my clients."

When confronted with these kinds of responses, what should you do as a coach? Ask the resisting professional to inquire whether his corporate clients are seeking customer feedback and whether they find that feedback useful. You know what the clients' answers will be to these questions. Of course they are getting client feedback. To gain maximum mileage from this technique, you must convince the professional to specify a client he will ask and set forth a time frame by which he will ask these questions. Then you must be sure to follow up to find out what the client said to him and use that information accordingly to build your case.

Another useful way to make your case is to relate the topic to the professional's field. As a former trial lawyer, I ask such specialists if they always make a point of talking with juries after a trial regardless of whether they win or lose. (Note: Some courts prohibit trial professionals from speaking to jurors after the trial.) The answer is almost always a resounding yes. The ones who say no aren't trial lawyers I want representing me. There is much to be learned from juror feedback. I then draw a parallel between juror feedback and client feedback. Why would you do it with jurors, but not with clients? I've not yet heard a compelling answer to that question. Thankfully, there are no prohibitions against professionals asking for feedback from their clients.

What else can be done to make the case for client feedback? Prepare a memo that is brief-like in form. Some professionals are more readily persuaded when they can look at the arguments in writing. An added benefit is the increased respect you, the proponent, will earn from partners if they think you write clearly and concisely.

Be sure to provide as much supporting documentation as you can gather. For example, it took one marketing director two years to persuade his firm to do client interviews. During that two-year period, he went to corporate counsel gatherings and asked them what they thought of law firms who asked them for feedback. Naturally, they told him they loved the idea. He also scoured the planet for and collected articles on the benefits of doing client interviews.

You can also collect war stories of the client relationships (and fees) preserved by seeking client feedback. A typical story goes something like this: During the interview the firm learned a major client was getting ready to fire the firm or had been in the process of systematically moving work elsewhere only to resurrect the relationship after learning the basis for its unhappiness. The greater the fees saved, the more persuasive the argument. One marketing director was able to show he saved one million dollars in fees as a result of doing one client interview.

In another case, a real estate specialist in the Midwest realized she was unwittingly sending a negative signal to clients and prospective clients. She would never have learned about it if she hadn't stepped outside her comfort zone and arranged a meeting with her client with nothing on her agenda except gathering client feedback. From this conversation with her client she learned that her client thought she was too busy to do the work. This professional was stunned. She inquired of the client what she did to give the client that impression. The client was unable to pinpoint any one thing, but she added that several of her employees reached the same conclusion about her work load. This professional resolved never again to complain about being busy. Instead, she would adopt the practice of dealing with every client as if she had all the time in the world to devote to the client, even though she might be incredibly busy.

For further data, consider AT&T, which was having trouble linking increases or decreases in customer satisfaction to market results. So, AT&T did a study, which was widely reported in business magazines such as *Fortune*. They found three things that helped explain these anomalies: (1) only very satisfied customers count; (2) other things besides price factor into customer thinking (things such as service and responsiveness); and (3) these scores must be measured relative to one's competitors. In other words, relative customer satisfaction has a high correlation to market results!

The implications for professionals are daunting. If you don't score the highest possible ratings with clients, you're vulnerable. Being satisfied isn't enough; clients must be *very* satisfied. If your competitors score higher than you, you're vulnerable. Even if you score very high on client satisfaction, but your competitor scores higher, you may still lose your client.

If you are an individual professional who can't get your firm to sanction client interviews, start doing them with your own clients. Then use the feedback from your clients to build a case for the firm doing them. One professional I worked with in Toronto did exactly that. When I sat down with him to find out how he would conduct the interviews, however, he had no questions prepared and had not identified the client he would do it with first. After some intense coaching, this professional conducted three client interviews during a two-month period, and was very glad that he did. In fact, he could not understand why he had not done this throughout his career.

I've seen the same thing happen with marketing directors. They spend so much energy just trying to secure firm buy-in for doing the interviews that they don't have the foggiest notion of the questions they want to ask. One marketing director of a medium-sized firm in the western U.S. realized she had no idea what questions she would ask if she ever got the green light for doing them. She also was stymied by resistance from the managing partner. She never considered trying to do these interviews with another professional in the firm who was willing to interview her clients and then use that experience as a springboard for doing them firm-wide.

Even total strangers can help us make the case for gathering client feedback. A personal experience I had is instructive. While flying to another city to conduct a client workshop and coaching program, I happened to sit next to the CEO of a California-based bar coding company. After telling him that I had practiced law for several years and that I am now coaching professionals of all kinds, including lawyers, he said, "Don't get me started on lawyers." He then proceeded to articulate, in excruciating detail, the things his current firm did that drove him crazy. Some of his feedback will sound familiar to those of you who are already doing client interviews.

He pointed out several deficiencies in his current firm. His company frequently acquired smaller bar coding companies. Hence, one of his objectives was always to keep the buying price low so he could increase shareholder value. He felt most lawyers were totally oblivious to his desire to increase shareholder value. More importantly, they didn't understand that he wanted his lawyer to play the bad guy during negotiations on pricing issues. Why? Because this CEO usually hired the owner to manage that portion of the operation and didn't want to start on poor terms with this future employee.

This CEO hated the revolving door of associates who worked with him on each new acquisition. Most of the associates provided to him didn't understand his business and how it makes money. Sometimes they lacked basic financial acumen, and other times they didn't understand his industry. He usually wound up having to educate most associates and pay the firm for the privilege. He loved it when he'd get an associate who understood all these issues, but invariably this associate would leave the firm. The next associate was not so well informed.

His ambivalence was representative of many clients: While dealing with a less favored associate he'd decide to fire the firm. Then when the deal was over, he'd forget about it until he got involved in the next acquisition. His frustrations would resurface and he'd again decide to fire his law firm once the next deal was over. This continued for more than a year. I asked him why he stayed with such a firm. His answer was that the firm helped him out of a personal pickle many years ago. That bought it a lot of good will. But, he added, "I've paid them far more than that in fees since then."

Two hours later, towards the end of the flight, he asked me, a total stranger, "Do you know of any good lawyers in my city?" I was astonished. This law firm was in the process of being fired, but it didn't know it because it hadn't asked. This story could just as easily have been about accountants or engineers or professionals of any kind. Don't let your firm make the same mistake.

*Demonstrate to your clients that you care
by following up on all your advice.*

11

FOLLOW UP ON YOUR
PROFESSIONAL ADVICE

HOW CAN I DEMONSTRATE TO MY CLIENTS
THAT I GENUINELY CARE?

I have found that following up on all the advice you give is
both a great service practice and an effective marketing
tool. Yet it is rarely used for either purpose with the frequency I would expect.

GREAT SERVICE PRACTICE

I'll bet you offer advice to your clients (and non-clients) every
day. I think most professionals would be surprised at how
much advice they offer during any given week. I'm struck by
how few ever feel the need to follow up on their advice. In my
view, following up on advice you give to others isn't just a
marketing skill; it's an essential service skill. How so? Well,
suppose you give a client some advice and fail to follow up to
see what she did with it. How do you know if the advice
worked for her in her unique circumstance? Unless you follow
up, you don't know. For all you know the advice didn't work.
Giving out advice that isn't used or doesn't work is lousy mar-

keting and it's sloppy service. Even if it does work, failing to follow up on your advice sends a very negative signal to your client or prospective client. It says, "I'm not terribly concerned about you and I'm not interested in learning how my advice turned out." In effect, you miss out on the learning. From now on, close the loop on whether or not it works. This applies to professionals in private practice and those working for a company. This practice is equally valuable to most inside advisors, such as firm marketing directors and information technology people. It applies to anyone who is in the business of giving advice to others, including most professional service providers!

I would estimate that the typical professional dispenses advice to between five and 20 people per week. Most of the recipients of this advice are clients, and some are not. This means the average advisor ought to be making five to 20 follow-up calls per week. Most of these calls will be to clients, some not. (By the way, the timing of your follow-up is critical. Don't wait two weeks to call your client if you know she will be using your advice tomorrow. Call tomorrow!) Professionals who do this overwhelmingly report how valuable it is to follow up. The client's favorable reaction surprises many professionals and strongly reinforces their motivation to do it over and over again. After three to four weeks of doing this consistently, many professionals find it has become a habit. Try it every day for a month and make it a habit.

The effects on the quality of professional services provided are pretty obvious. Assume there are two equally capable professionals: one who routinely follows up on all advice he gives and the other who follows up intermittently on the advice he gives. Fast forward one year: Which of these two will be a better professional service provider? Obviously, the one who consistently follows up on advice will be much better than the one who does it sporadically. In fact, one of the pronounced differences between good professionals and great ones is that great professionals follow up on their advice far more frequently and consistently than do good professionals.

Some of you might be thinking this is a good idea, but "I just don't have the time." If that's your thinking, you are saying a great deal about your priorities. This has to be important enough to you that you resolve to make the time for it. If you don't make the time to follow up on your advice, you'll never be a great advisor. Even if you reach the point that you don't want any more clients, if you have pursued this habit of following up on advice, you are much more likely to be fully engaged quickly, and you are much more likely to have a group of clients you really want to have.

One professional I have been coaching became so convinced of the value of this practice that he purchased contact management software to keep track of his advice and the follow-up it spawns. He loaded it onto his computer and immediately began adding two to three names to it each week. He is using it to track follow-up calls with clients. He has already made a number of follow-up calls, and his clients' reactions have been very favorable. He also feels more on top of things. Before, he was sporadic about following up on advice. He now makes a point of trying to find out more about how his clients plan on using his advice. He has found it habit forming—once started, it built its own momentum. It's the first thing he thinks about when he gets off the phone with a client. He asks himself, "Did this phone call generate the need for any follow-up?" If the answer is yes, he calendars an action into his contact management software.

In case you're wondering, I do this extensively. I make dozens of suggestions to my clients each week and follow up on nearly all of them. I am fanatical about the follow-up on my advice. Much of it works. Sometimes it works better than I envisioned, and sometimes it doesn't. I've learned that advice that works great for one person may never be tried by another. The same is true for you. Just because one client loved your advice doesn't mean that any of the next three clients will like the same advice. They may never try it or they may try it but then conclude it doesn't work. The point is that following up regularly makes for happier clients, more business, and a more learned professional.

GREAT MARKETING TOOL

In my view, the most compelling marketing reason for adopting this practice is that it demonstrates your care and concern to the client. An employment lawyer had helped one of her clients design an employee drug testing procedure for screening prospective employees. With the help of her coach, this lawyer devised a game plan for following up with the general counsel at her client firm. Her goal was to observe the testing protocol at one of the client's plants, and she was prepared to do this without charge as a way of delivering value. There were dozens of other plants that might also be in need of an audit. If it worked she could charge for these additional site reviews. After some prompting from her coach, she called general counsel and made the offer. General counsel declined the offer, but the very call itself demonstrated the employment lawyer's care and concern for the client's well-being.

There is another good reason why it's an effective marketing tool—to stay in contact with your client. This works very well with dormant clients and is particularly valuable to project or case-based professionals, who often struggle to find reasons why they should re-contact a client whom they are no longer representing in an ongoing matter. For example, a consultant had helped her client design a corporate compliance program. During a meeting with her coach, she realized that it had been some time since she had spoken to the client and she did not know whether the client ever implemented the program she designed. Soon thereafter, she called the client and, as predicted, won kudos for following up. It also turns out the client had not actually implemented the program. He asked her to help him get the program up and running and insisted on being billed for her time. The dollars she generated from her follow-up were modest. The goodwill was priceless.

I'm betting that as you read this chapter there were several clients you thought about who deserve your follow-up. Why not call them today? You and your clients will be glad you did.

There are a multitude of people in your life who stand willing to help you, but you must be willing to ask.

12

GENERATING ENDLESS REFERRALS

How Do I Generate More Referrals?

Ideally, your work is so exceptional you are generating unprompted referrals from clients and friends. Unprompted referrals are rare, in part because we send off some very negative signals to clients and friends when we're asked how we're doing. Many professionals respond by saying how busy they are. That's definitely the wrong answer. The nonverbal message you're sending is "Go away. I'm too busy to take on more work." That kind of response will lower the number of unprompted referrals you might receive. The best rainmakers in any profession give people the impression that they have all the time in the world for someone—even when they don't.

SAY THANK YOU EARLY AND OFTEN

One easy way to generate referrals is to always say "thanks" to those people who provide actual and attempted referrals. All of us learned to say thank you before we were weaned off diapers. Even though this point is obvious, several professionals from each workshop I do on this topic sheepishly admit they forget to say thanks. The reason: They don't write a note to themselves to say thanks. What you might not have learned is to say thanks two or three times. These thank you's might be spread out over a month. Here is how they might unfold: Call 1: "Thanks. Your friend called me and we are set to meet on Tuesday. I'll let you know how it goes." Call 2 a week later: "Thanks again. We met on Tuesday and she will get back to me shortly. I'll let you know what she decides." Call 3 another week later: "Wanted to close the loop and let you know she didn't hire us. But I appreciate your thinking of us."

I've found it useful to thank people with something more tangible than a phone call. With your best referral sources, you might send a hand-written thank you note or a small gift, or offer to buy breakfast or lunch as a more tangible way of saying thanks.

Unprompted Referrals

Very few professionals know how to receive an unprompted referral effectively. An unprompted referral is client-initiated, spontaneous, and unpredictable. Most fumble the opportunity, either because they don't know how to develop it or they fail to follow up. Here are some common situations where referrals arise:

- Your client says there is someone else in his company you should meet; or
- Your client says there is someone else in another company you should meet; or
- Your friend from college who works at IBM says, "You really ought to meet Becky because she is the corporate counterpart for what you do"; or
- Your friend/relative suggests you get in touch with someone who needs a professional service provider; or
- Your partner suggests you meet with one of his clients or friends.

Some referral sources only give you the names of people they know who are actively looking for a professional service provider. Others simply make the introduction and make no effort to determine the need of the referral for your services. Many professionals I've coached have had clients give them the names of others to contact. Most are uneducated about what to do with those opportunities. There are a variety of ways to advance the relationship. Here are six outcomes (shown in the figure below) that should be considered in these situations:

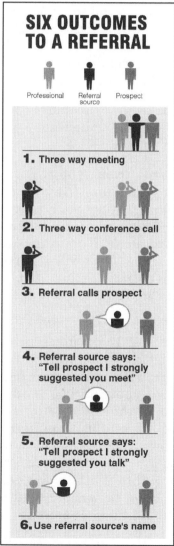

SIX OUTCOMES TO A REFERRAL

Professional | Referral source | Prospect

1. Three way meeting

2. Three way conference call

3. Referral calls prospect

4. Referral source says: "Tell prospect I strongly suggested you meet"

5. Referral source says: "Tell prospect I strongly suggested you talk"

6. Use referral source's name

Six Outcomes to a Referral

1. See whether your client is willing to participate, and perhaps even arrange, a three-way meeting. A client's willingness to get involved at this level shows greater commitment.

2. See whether your client is willing to participate in, and even arrange, a three-way conference call. Sometimes a three-way meeting isn't feasible because each person is based in a different city. This kind of introduction still shows significant commitment to helping you.

3. See whether your client will call the referral first to let her know you will be calling and urge the person to meet with you when you call. This increases your odds.

4. During the call with your client, ask if it's alright to say to the referral that he "strongly suggested we meet." Then during your call to the referral, you can repeat that exact language. Again, this increases your odds of a meeting.

5. During the call with your client, ask him or her to support you telling the referral that he or she "strongly suggests we talk." Then during your call to the referral, you can repeat that exact language. It is less clear if that means nothing more than a phone call or if it means a meeting might be appropriate.

6. The last (and most common outcome sought by most professionals) is permission to use your referral source's name during the call to the referral. If you go this route and have not taken the time to understand details of the referral's problem, you are not giving yourself a chance to put your best foot forward.

Think of these six outcomes as being a way to gauge commitment. The level of commitment your referral source is making decreases as you move down the list.

Frequently, professionals don't even realize the first five options are available to them. That means they hang up the phone, or end the meeting, without gauging their referral source's level of commitment to making the introduction. Rarely are your clients sophisticated in how to make the introduction for you. Without prompting, most will gravitate to the last option. More often than not, this is a missed opportunity to increase commitment and the likelihood of a meeting.

An accountant, Howard, got a call from an executive search consultant, Sara, who had referred him work previously. Sara had learned that one of Howard's clients was talking to a competing accounting firm about hiring another auditor. Sara gave Howard the name of the CFO, Ruth, and suggested he call. Aside from falling low on the commitment scale, Howard was unsure about how to best proceed. With help from his coach, he devised a list of questions to ask, including: "Are you still looking for auditors?" If yes, his goal was to secure a meeting with Ruth. If no, he was prepared to see if she was willing to meet so he could find out more about her business.

PROMPTING REFERRALS

More and more professionals I work with want to learn how to prompt referrals from their most ardent supporters. A prompted referral is one where you choose the timing and that is initiated by the professional after planning out how he or she will ask. If you have the chutzpah to ask for referrals frequently, you can build a very healthy practice. The most common kind of prompted referral comes from satisfied clients. Sometimes, names are volunteered, but other times you must ask. There are very few professionals I work with who don't have at least one staunch champion on their list of clients. Most don't ask for fear of looking like the proverbial life insurance salesman who slides a piece of paper across the desk and asks for the names of six other people you know. It need not be that way.

Since most professionals haven't received any instruction on how to approach the task of asking for referrals, their effort, due to ignorance, ends up being far too general. A tax professional might ask, "Charlie, do you know of any other people who might want to meet me?" I've learned that such an approach rarely works. Aside from it feeling uncomfortable, it's also ineffective. It's so uncomfortable that many professionals will totally give up on the idea of asking for referrals. That's a mistake too. Just because doing it ineffectively hasn't worked before doesn't mean it will never work.

A more effective method is to ask a more specific question. Your odds of gaining a referral skyrocket if you ask for specifics! Our tax professional above might ask, "Can you think of any fellow CFOs who are struggling with a large tax bill?" or "Can you think of any fellow CFOs who are struggling with messy tax issues?" or "Charlie, do you have any former college classmates who have been griping about their current tax situation?" These specific questions are more likely to prompt people to think of a name.

Another variation when talking with your partner might be, "Have any of your clients shared struggles with messy tax issues?" There are a wide variety of ways to craft the question, and there is no magic language. The key is to write out a very specific question you feel comfortable asking and then ask it.

If the client's answer is yes, your goal is to find out more about her knowledge of the problem, rather than immediately chase the name. Only after spending some time on defining and understanding what the referral source knows about the problem should you ask the ultimate question regarding a referral. At that point, I would suggest you ask something such as "Would you be comfortable introducing us?" or "Do you think this person would be open to our meeting?" or "Do you think this person is at a point where she's ready to meet with me?" You might preface the question with this statement: "Gee, that sounds like something that perfectly matches my expertise. Would you be comfortable introducing us?"

Don't write off the notion that an intensely loyal client who hired you while he was at another company can't send you referrals, even though he is required to use the incumbent professional service firm at his new company. An expert in Canada had tried unsuccessfully for several years to regain work he had done for a bank while with his previous firm. There were several people at the bank who wanted to hire him, but not unless his new firm moved some of the firm's accounts over to the bank. His former firm had done this, but his new firm would not. What should he do? Go for referrals. He had an impressive history of delivering outstanding service with the bank and several people who would love to work with him again. Many professionals face this situation in some form or another. In fact, the person he knew at the bank became his top referral source. It led to a referral from the bank that yielded $60,000 in fees. The question he asked his contact was: "Are there any borrowers you are working with you'd feel comfortable introducing me to?"

Once you've obtained the name, you must be vigilant about following up on the lead. If you do everything right, but fail to follow up, all your efforts will come to naught.

Professionals spring surprises on their clients every month in the form of their bills.

13

USING BILLS AS MARKETING TOOLS

How Do I Get Marketing Mileage from My Bills?

Professional services are intangible. Given that obvious fact, how do your clients draw conclusions about the work you've performed for them? These conclusions are drawn from their interactions with you. In fact, any time any person (not just a client) perceives some aspect of your firm, that person forms a conscious or subconscious impression of the quality and value of your services. One often overlooked interaction clients use to gauge the quality of your services is your bills. You can use your bills as a marketing tool.

Ideally, your clients never challenge your bills. It's the rare professional or firm that can say that. Often, the surprise and the hassles it entails are preventable by doing a better job of managing client expectations.

Clients hate surprises. Yet one of the most unwelcome surprises you can spring on a client is a bill that is larger than expected. Why is that? Because most clients have budgets and internal reasons why staying within their budgets is imperative. Professionals are incredibly uninformed about how their clients are affected by a surprise bill. Since most clients have to live within a world of budgets and cash flows, your surprise may rain intense scrutiny down upon them. Predictability is highly desired.

Can you think of a bill you sent out recently that was much higher than either you or the client expected it to be? How did you handle it? Most professionals handle surprise bills poorly. They send out the bill and wait to see if the client complains. Doing so is at best a squandered opportunity for relationship building. The best rainmakers call their clients in advance of sending the bill and tell them the dollar amount. They often suggest a meeting to go over the bill in person and get some feedback. In short, they use the surprise bill as an opportunity to begin a dialogue with the client. Most professionals are so afraid of discussing fees that they do almost anything to avoid having to make that call. The net result is a weakened relationship. Burying your head in the sand is nearly always the worst thing you can do.

One professional successfully used the billing process to make the charges more predictable for the client and to ensure prompt payment. She visited the client's accountant in another state and spent the better part of a day understanding the client's accounting system and learning exactly what was needed to pay the bills and exactly how and when the check runs occurred. She then set up a system that transmitted bills in electronic form in time to coordinate with the client's requirements and the timing of the check runs. She even gave the client authority to edit and write the bills down or up to a certain modest extent in order to ensure that the bill, as edited, would be paid promptly instead of held for discussion.

I received a call from a client who had sent out a bill to his client that was higher than expected. Since it was too late to call beforehand, he asked what the firm could do. Quite a bit. I urged this professional to impress on the relationship manager the need to call the client and ask whether he had any questions. Depending on the kind of answers received, I suggested they meet in person to go over the bill item by item.

While preparing for the meeting, reflect on how your professional services fit within the big picture of the client's business. For example, if your bill reflects the research needed to ensure that your client eliminated an entire 18-person department without any legal action taken against the company, then say so in the bill. Even bills that aren't surprises are given short shrift. In my view, every bill that goes out has the potential to double as a brochure.

Many professionals claim to be too busy to undertake marketing. They are the same people who say doing great work is the best form of marketing. I agree that doing great work is a valuable form of marketing, but I also believe many of these same professionals send out bills that don't reflect how valuable their work is. What a missed opportunity! How much time do you spend editing your bills each month to convey the sense of effort you expended on behalf of your client? Many professionals think they are only keeping track of their time, not adding perceived value. They are dead wrong!

During your next practice group meeting, try this: Bring one or two bills that are scheduled to go out in the next billing cycle and split up into two groups. Have each group rewrite the bill as if they were Madison Avenue advertising executives. Then compare the best aspects of both bills and see what you've got. I guarantee you could make dramatic improvements to your bills. This one action could have a profound effect on the client's willingness to pay the bill and increase his or her appreciation of what you are doing. Here are elements of an effective bill:

1. AGGREGATE INFORMATION ON THE BILL IN THE WAY THE CLIENT WANTS IT. If she wants you to group your time by matter, then do so. Client needs in this area vary widely, so make sure you are clear at the beginning of the engagement about what he or she wants.

2. PRESENT THE BILL IN THE FORM AND FREQUENCY THE CLIENT DESIRES. If the client needs your bill by the fifth of each month because he uses it as a basis for a report he does on the tenth, make sure he gets it in sufficient time. Some

clients need bills sent to them monthly; others may want bills more or less frequently.

3. BE VIGILANT ABOUT DISCREPANCIES IN THE BILL. For example, avoid entries reporting that the associate met with the partner for .5 hours, and that the partner spent .75 hours in the same meeting.

4. CONVEY A DETAILED DESCRIPTION OF THE WORK DONE AND THE VALUE PROVIDED TO THE CLIENT. Obviously this task is made easier if you remember to record your time immediately after you complete the task. Even so, professionals have a hard time with this because they really don't know what their clients value. This requires a dialogue with the client about big picture issues.

5. SEE WHETHER THE CLIENT HAS ANY REQUIREMENTS OF CONFIDENTIALITY. For example, he or she may not want the bill opened by an assistant or others within the company.

6. WATCH FOR TYPOGRAPHICAL AND MATHEMATICAL ERRORS. Clients frequently cannot gauge the quality of our services on a technical scale, but they sure notice if we misspell something.

7. USE QUALITY PAPER. Sending your statement of professional fees to clients on anything less than high grade paper or using a dot matrix printer communicates this nonverbal message: "This statement isn't very important, so take your time for payment." It may also cause the client to wonder if the quality of the work you are doing is comparable to the quality of your statement.

8. STATE WHEN PAYMENT IS DUE. This may seem obvious, but clients are quite sophisticated and will use your failure to state when the bill is due as license to put it off for 60 to 180 days or more.

Sending out bills is a huge opportunity, rather than a chore that keeps coming up every month. On your next bill, spend the time to add words that convey value from the client's perspective and see if you notice quicker payment.

The best time to seek payment on the bill is when it's less than 30 days overdue. The second best time is today.

14

COLLECTING YOUR FEES
AT YEAR-END

How Do I Avoid Year-End Collection Problems?

Many professionals get uncomfortable when they have to talk to their clients about fees. If you're not one of them, read no further. For the rest of us, however, it's a different story. It can get even worse when clients are habitually paying their fees late. As a result, professionals tend to put off the inevitable conversation until several months or the whole year has passed. That is a sloppy business practice. It also makes the task of collecting the fees much harder than it needs to be. Too many professionals get pulled away from their practices in the month of December because they are busy making last-ditch efforts to collect the fees clients owe them. If I measured the wasted time and energy professionals spend worrying about collecting fees, it would dwarf the actual time and energy needed to collect those same fees.

Collecting fees is a year-round and ongoing responsibility. When you let your clients pay late, you wreak havoc on the cash flow of your firm. In extreme cases, your delay could jeopardize the health of the firm. Don't wait until December to start collecting.

The solutions are obvious. If that's true, why is the December collection problem so pervasive? Some say it's procrastination, but that is just a symptom. The root cause is the fear and distaste with which most professionals view the task. Most professionals would rather watch "Lassie" reruns than collect from a slow-paying client. Another major reason for their discomfort is not knowing how to do it. What follows are ways to collect comfortably. I won't pretend to prescribe a one-size-fits-all approach, just some guidelines that work.

When Is the Best Time to Collect Your Fees?

That's easy, when the receivable first becomes categorized as overdue. When your invoice is more than 30 days old, pick up the phone and call your client. That means if the bill went out on May 1 you should be making a phone call by mid-June if payment hasn't been received. No excuses. "I'm too busy working on projects" is a lame excuse for not making this call. Your building landlord doesn't cut you slack for not paying rent because you're "too busy working." A professional service firm is a business, and not a financing vehicle for its clients. Clients will respect professionals who treat their own business as seriously as the clients treat theirs.

How Should You Begin and What Should You Say?

Of the professionals who put this task off, I'd estimate that a large proportion do so because they are not exactly sure how to begin the call. Here is one way to start the conversation: "We sent you an invoice on February 20th and I wanted to be sure you have received it." (If you get the proverbial "the check's in the mail" response, and you're wary, ask the client for verification of the date the check was cut.) If the client says, "Yes, we received the bill," then enlist your client's help in getting it paid. It's always helpful to operate on the assumption that your client is willing to help you get paid until proven otherwise.

Assume your contact is never the cause for the holdup in payment and instead assume it's the accounts payable system.

If your client is a one-person show, assume she just forgot about it and was understandably swamped by the press of other business. If you want, make the firm's management the bad guys. You might say, "My partners/finance committee are giving me grief because of this unpaid invoice; is there anything you can do to help expedite payment?" Notice this is a question rather than a demand. Most clients will be embarrassed and apologetic. If the check is large enough (where it's feasible), I might even propose to meet with the client to review the bill in person and collect payment.

WHO SHOULD MAKE THE CALL?

Many large firms have administrative staff whose job it is to collect unpaid invoices. You can certainly rely on them up to a point. Once it gets moderately overdue, though, I'd suggest the professional make this call rather than the accounting department. Why? It's a chance to build the relationship. If you don't have a relationship in which you can have this conversation, then you have much bigger problems than an aging receivable. Handled well, the task of collecting fees will actually strengthen your client relationship. Handle this task poorly, however, and you give the client the impression that your fees are more important than the relationship. The more pressure you're feeling to collect, the more prone you are to slip into heavy-handedness. All the more reason not to wait until the last minute.

*When raising fees, focus on the value
you're delivering to your client.*

15

RAISING YOUR FEES

HOW DO I RAISE MY FEES WITHOUT LOSING THE CLIENT?

The topic of raising fees always sparks great interest among my clients. There is no one-size-fits-all approach. I strongly suggest, however, that when you decide to raise your fees, you make every effort at having this conversation in person with your best clients. If that's not feasible, a phone call works better than anything in writing. With the clients you're not as concerned about keeping, a letter will do.

This topic has come up frequently with clients lately. I will share with you some of the ideas I share with them.

First, make very sure you're worth the increase. Clients aren't stupid. If they can find another advisor who can provide the same service quality as you do for what you're currently charging them, your chances for a substantial increase aren't good. In most cases, corporate officers are dealing with a handful (or dozens) of professionals around the country (or world) who are hired to do the same thing you are doing, so they have a basis for comparison that you don't.

It's very difficult to know whether you are worth the increase unless you've been gathering feedback all along on how you're doing. There are very few professionals who make it a regular practice to find out how their service levels compare to their competition. If you don't get that kind of client feedback, it will be difficult to gauge your value. One question you could ask is, "How does our work for you compare to that of other firms you work with around the country?"

A Denver trial lawyer tried this with a large client who was chronically slow (90 days or more) to pay the firm's invoices. He started off his discussion with the client by asking him for feedback on how they were doing. He also asked what he could do to become even easier to do business with. The client appreciated this approach so much that he responded in kind. The lawyer asked for help on how to speed up payment on the firm's invoices and learned a way to secure payment within 30 days. From a cash flow perspective, getting paid 60 days sooner is almost as good as a fee increase.

Most professionals like to think it's their sheer technical brilliance that enables them to charge the rates they do. That's rarely the case. In most instances, your technical skills are a commodity. There are other things, however, that move your service beyond commodity status. To name a few, consider your intimate knowledge of the client's business, your industry knowledge, and your knowledge of the client's idiosyncrasies (for example, they will never accept charges for sending faxes or copies).

Another factor that might justify a fee increase is speed. As discussed earlier, not enough professionals realize how important speed is to clients. I've heard plenty of stories about firms that are very responsive and speedy when the relationship first starts, but then the firm's service levels drop over time.

Sometimes clients will pay a premium for speed. To find out whether or not this might be the case, ask your clients. This can spark a very productive dialogue. You may be surprised by the answer and you'll probably learn a great deal in the process. For example, if it takes you one month (on average) to help a client close a deal and the next closest competitor takes three months, you're probably swamped with work. And you're probably undercharging your client even though at first blush you're offering the "same" service. You ought to be looking at raising your rates. If the speed at which you work allows your client to close deals faster, it also allows your client to generate cash flow sooner. Your lack of speed can work against you too. I see many professionals with such a neurotic need for perfection that it takes them forever to produce a finished product. As I recently warned one consultant: "Your need for perfection is going to bump up against the marketplace's need for speed and timeliness."

Here is another positive approach you might consider to raising your fees. If you want to achieve a certain hourly rate, the operative question to ask your client is: "What would we have to do for you so that you feel we are worth $250 (or whatever rate you want to charge) per hour?"

One professional, let's call him Bob, tried this approach with his client and it worked. The client agreed to allow Bob to charge his standard hourly rate and then give her a 10 percent reduction. The total added fees Bob will earn during the course of just one year exceeds $50,000. The lesson learned by Bob was that his client wanted to be able to go back to her boss and say, "I got us a 10 percent reduction." Bob also learned from this discussion that his rates were still below the rates of another professional service firm the client worked with.

Even if you get an answer such as: "There is nothing you can do," you're no worse off than you were before asking. Regardless of the answer, this question will almost certainly spark a discussion with your clients about delivering value unlike anything you've had before.

Whatever you do, avoid an adversarial approach at all costs. Too many professionals take such an approach to the whole issue of raising fees, which is very ineffective. Rather than approaching the client by saying, "We must raise our rates or else . . ," it's more effective to say, "I've got a problem that I need your help with. . . ." Another lawyer's recent experience is instructive. Dennis is a real estate lawyer in a large firm that does major real estate deals for a huge grocery chain. Dennis' fees had been kept steady for five years and he had been getting pressure from his firm to tell the client he must raise his rates or else. A year before, Dennis and his managing partner flew out and met with the client in another state for the express purpose of changing the fee structure. The client wouldn't budge.

I met with Dennis recently on another issue, but the internal pressures on him to raise his rates with this client were enormous so he asked for ideas. I suggested he take the "I've got a problem that I need your help with" approach, and he was amazed with the results.

He initially dreaded raising the issue of fees. Dennis was so nervous about bringing up the issue that he organized my suggestions and his thoughts on paper after our meeting in preparation for a call to his client. He also made a list of items that demonstrated the value he had been delivering. As it turned out, the client called him on a work-related matter, then asked, "Is everything going okay?" That was his opening, and he took it. Dennis said he'd like to raise the issue of fees. In part, he said, "My rate is discounted 30 percent. It's adversely affecting my career. I'm devoting my life to helping your business succeed. I'm catching major heat from my firm. I need your help. Can we explore ways to make this a win-win?" He also went through the list of actions that demonstrated his value to the client.

The client, the same one who said "no dice" the year before, said, "You know what. . . . I agree with your points. Submit a proposal. We'll consider it and make changes as of the beginning of the month." As it turned out, his client was willing to champion a request for an increase, but he needed ammunition to sell it internally. In the end, Dennis secured an increase. More importantly, the sense of relief he felt after it was all over was worth more than the increase.

Most professionals are like Dennis; they dread asking for fee increases. Those who muster up the courage to raise the issue with clients are miles ahead of those who are too fearful of what the client might say or think. With the right approach, you'll be rewarded with higher fees, better understanding of what the client values, and a stronger relationship. Makes you wonder why we resist this so strenuously, doesn't it?

SELLING SKILLS

Think in detail about what outcome you want before you head off to your next marketing meeting.

16

TEN FATAL SELLING ERRORS PROFESSIONALS MAKE

WHAT ARE THE MOST COMMON MISTAKES MADE?

I've witnessed many marketing successes and many marketing failures during my career. The failures tend to have common roots.

TALKING MORE THAN LISTENING

We're lucky that clients hire us at all, given our penchant for talking. On the one hand, it's not surprising that we talk so much, since that is ordinarily one of our strengths as professionals. In the selling arena it's a major weakness. If you're talking, you can't be learning much about what the client needs. Sometimes professionals tell me they have a hard time marketing because they are painfully shy or introverted. I tell them that's great! When they inquire why I think that's so wonderful, I explain to them that some of the best rainmakers on the planet are introverts, which means they are usually great listeners.

I normally work with firms for 30 days or more. At the end of the coaching period, I ask them for feedback on the program, particularly the coaching. The comment I delight in hearing most often from my clients is, "The only thing I am doing differently from before is listening better to what the client needs." I usually respond, just as I tell my law students every year, that listening is the foundational skill to great professional service. It's also the foundational skill to great marketing.

GOING TO MARKETING MEETINGS UNPREPARED, NOT KNOWING ABOUT THE INDUSTRY, COMPANY, OR PERSON

Perhaps the largest single failing of professionals going into marketing meetings is their lack of preparation. If a lawyer goes into trial unprepared, the result is losing. If you go into a business development meeting unprepared, the result is rejection. The better your preparation, the smaller the chance of rejection. Nearly everyone finds rejection unpleasant yet won't do the single most important thing to head off rejection, and that's to prepare. I will summarize the three things every professional should do before any marketing meeting: (1) Write out the needs of the person or persons you are meeting; (2) Write down three to four questions you hope to ask the client; and (3) Write out the outcome you hope to achieve from the meeting. I will elaborate on these three things in the next chapter.

A banking lawyer, who was also the department chairman and a highly accomplished rainmaker, had prepared extensively with his coach for a meeting with a prospective client. The meeting went so well he walked out of it with work and the promise of more to come. He learned several lessons from this meeting, but the one that stood out for him the most was that, while you can have a pretty good meeting without being prepared, you can have a great meeting when you're well-prepared. Many professionals I work with have been to many marketing meetings, but rarely have they gone into these meetings fully, or even partially, prepared. When professionals experience what it feels like to go into a marketing meeting fully prepared, most are transformed permanently. It becomes a self-reinforcing experience.

Failing to Consider the Personal Needs
of the Contact

Personal needs influence more sales than almost any other competitive factor. Yet, very rarely will a room full of professional service providers articulate even one personal need when asked: "What does this person need?" For example, the CEO of a prospective client cares about the stock price, but she cares even more about her stock options.

Personal needs include such things as saving time, having fun, maintaining control, avoiding surprises, hearing bad news early, and needing to be right or at least not told you're wrong. I persuaded one professional to gather feedback from her existing clients about why she was hired. She was surprised to hear one of her clients say that she was hired in part because they thought she'd be fun to work with. This same professional asked another client about a month later why she was hired. She was shocked to learn that the second client considered that to be a deciding factor as well.

Focusing On What They Need (More Work) Rather
Than on What the Prospective Client Needs

I always ask professionals what their clients need and it is surprising how often they start telling me what they, the professionals, need instead. Selling is about seeing that your client's needs are met. If your primary motive is what you'll get from someone, you will limit your effectiveness.

Not Asking for a Single Advance
During Their Meeting

An advance is the next step the client is willing to take to move the sale forward. A patent lawyer in a Midwestern firm arranged a meeting with the subsidiary of a company for which he used to be in-house patent counsel. His meeting with this general counsel went pretty well until the end of the meeting, at which time the general counsel said, "I will get back to you." He didn't know what to do with that response. This meeting ended like many meetings he'd had with other prospective clients. If not for a debriefing with his coach, I predict this lawyer would have continued to finish many more meetings the same way. The question put to him was, "What will you do in one or two weeks if she doesn't call you?" He immediately got the point. He and his coach discussed how he would handle that situation differently next time. He could have responded with a question, "If I don't hear from you by the end of the week, is it okay if I call you?"

SEEKING AN ADVANCE THAT IS TOO AMBITIOUS

Even after professionals learn to secure an advance, they still misapply the concept. The most typical goal most professionals have as they head into meetings is to get work. That's not very likely to happen at a first meeting. The analogy to dating is quite apt: You don't walk up to a stranger and ask for his or her hand in marriage. Generally, most professionals try to go too fast. Move more slowly, perhaps by looking for a chance to give advice to the prospective client and get his or her permission to follow up and see how the advice worked. This allows them to "try before they buy."

FAILING TO WRITE THREE TO FOUR QUESTIONS YOU WILL ASK BEFORE THE MEETING

I'd be shocked if more than 10 percent of the professionals I work with actually take this step. Those who do always find that this kind of increased preparation pays huge dividends. The most commonly reported benefits are greater comfort level in the meeting and great spontaneity. If nothing else, writing out questions tends to stimulate curiosity about someone and gets us outside the "what's in it for me" mindset that pervades too many marketing meetings. This error is closely tied to talking more than listening. I've found you're more likely to commit the first error (failure to listen) if you don't write out questions.

SPEAKING IN PLATITUDES INSTEAD OF FACTS

Instead of an attorney saying, "We staff our cases leanly," he might say, "We were able to represent twice the number of co-defendants with half the number of professionals in that case." Instead of saying, "We are technologically sophisticated," say "Our firm can send out draft documents to four people who work for our client in four different word processing formats" or "Every professional and para-professional in our firm has a portable laptop computer." Every professional should reflect on his or her work experience and have at least three to five notable examples of achievement as samples of his or her work. These examples should demonstrate how good you are, rather than you having to toot your own horn.

KNOWING DANGEROUSLY LITTLE
ABOUT BUYER BEHAVIOR PATTERNS

One professional from the Midwest knew he made a great impression on a prospective client when she told him that she wanted him to help her company. This professional figured that he had all but made the sale. The reality was quite different. The person he met was in the marketing department and had only minimal influence on the decision makers in the company. What he needed to do was coach this person to make the sale internally.

The former in-house patent lawyer I mentioned earlier—the one who had a meeting with the general counsel—also knew the chief engineer at the spin-off company and called him. He asked the engineer to put in a good word for him with the general counsel. That's a wasted call. He should have rehearsed his engineering friend (and a champion for getting him in the door) on how to describe his talents to the general counsel. He should also have learned about the general counsel's needs through his contact.

DEALING POORLY WITH CLIENT OBJECTIONS

Nearly everyone has heard "Your fees are too high" or "We already have an expert in that field." Rather than rolling out your standard answer to the objection, look at it as a chance to gather valuable data from the marketplace. If someone says to you, "We already have that covered," immediately let go of your attachment to getting this person as a client and instead view it as a chance to gather market research and build the relationship. Remember, not every sales call results in a sale. Later on, your contact may call you with work.

Keep asking questions until you find a need,
and then work toward an advance.

17

AVOID RANDOM ACTS OF LUNCH

HOW CAN I AVOID WASTING MY MARKETING EFFORT
IN RANDOM, UNPLANNED ACTIONS?

Most professionals know exactly how to handle the technical aspects of their work. If they didn't, we wouldn't hire them. By contrast, most don't know exactly how to prepare for meetings with prospective clients because it's never been taught to them. I'd even predict that most of you went into one of the professions so you could AVOID marketing and selling! If you define selling as meeting client needs, it's not as tortuous as you might think.

This chapter will set forth a structure on how to "sell" in a way that provides value to the client and leaves you feeling comfortable, natural, and focused. If you apply this simple method, I can emphatically state you will experience greater success. It's been battle tested by thousands of professionals during the 12 years I've been doing this work.

Every firm has professionals with varying degrees of commitment to marketing. Some are rainmakers who engage in at least one or more marketing meetings per day. The average professional might have one or two meetings per week or fewer. There are a large numbers of professionals I've worked with who have never been to a single marketing meeting. All three types can benefit from applying the ideas in this chapter. Think of it as a checklist of what you can do to prepare for a sales meeting.

AVOID RANDOM ACTS OF LUNCH

These meetings are often (but not always) held over lunch. Regardless of the venue, I'd estimate that the typical professional wastes three to five hours each month because he or she heads off to meetings with little or no meaningful preparation. The troubling part is that most professionals genuinely believe meetings in which they "wing it" constitute effective selling. In truth, these meetings are little more than what I call "Random Acts of Lunch." Many professionals I've worked with admit that most of their lunches (and other marketing meetings) are random. You can have a good meeting without preparation, but you'll improve your chances for success immeasurably if you prepare.

When I ask firm leaders how many minutes the average professional spends preparing for a routine business development meeting (not full-blown "beauty contests"), the typical answer is "None." That's ironic because many professionals have an inordinate fear of rejection. Yet there is often a direct link between how well you prepare for a meeting and the likelihood of rejection. If it's helpful, think of focused preparation as a rejection-avoidance strategy. Showing up unprepared is also an insult to the prospective client because the messages you're sending are: "You're not important" and "Your time is not as valuable as mine."

FIRST THINGS FIRST: DO YOUR HOMEWORK

Let's start with a blinding flash of the obvious: Do your homework. Many professionals know they should do homework, but almost no one actually does it. Not many professionals have figured out that you can use preparation as a competitive advantage and differentiator. Given the ubiquity of company websites, I consider it "marketing malpractice" for a professional to head into a meeting with a potential client without first checking the client's website. On page 275 at the end of this book is a list of ideas and resources to be pursued as part of your preparation. It's much better to prepare thoroughly for one client meeting per month than to wing it with ten prospective clients each month. Many professionals report increased confidence when they go into meetings armed with useful information. In some situations, preparation will take 10 minutes; in other instances it might require several days of thoughtful due diligence. Once you've done your research it's time to get even more focused.

Here is a brief overview of the three things I want you to write out on the worksheet on page 279 at the end of this book before you head off to your next meeting. Let me repeat, these things should be written down BEFORE you go to your meeting.

1. NEEDS—Write out the personal needs and fears of whomever you are meeting. When I ask professionals what they think the prospect needs, too many start telling me what they, the professionals, need! That's a very big mistake. Prospective clients aren't interested in what you need. Considering another's needs will differentiate you as more empathic than your competitors. The more empathy you are able to demonstrate, the better the meeting. Here are some personal needs you might write down on your blank page: "Control," "Looking good to the boss," "Minimal time spent supervising the matter," and "Avoiding surprises."

Consult with a partner or your firm's marketing director if you are having difficulty thinking of personal needs. Remember the needs of head of sales are going to be different from the needs of the CEO. Many top-flight service professionals get a cold shoulder from one company representative on an idea that would have been very well-received by another. If you're talking to a CEO, he's most likely to be interested in "big picture" issues, whereas an operational leader is more likely to be interested in the details of her division.

2. QUESTIONS—Write out three or four questions you might ask during the meeting. When I ask an audience of professionals to place where they think a professional's selling behavior falls on a continuum from "ask" at one end to "tell" at the other end, most think it falls towards the "tell" end of the spectrum. The discipline of writing out questions can profoundly impact your mindset around what you're there for. If you want to build a great relationship, ask more questions. As I tell clients, "Whoever asks the most thoughtful questions wins." It also demonstrates to the client that you're prepared and understand his or her business.

Most professionals are reticent about preparing a list of questions. One enthusiastic professional I coached agreed to fax me a list of questions he intended to ask during an upcoming meeting. When I received the fax I chuckled because it didn't contain a single question, only talking points. I asked him to convert every point into a question. Contrary to popular belief, *telling is not selling.*

3. ADVANCES—Write down possible outcomes you'd like to see happen at the conclusion of your phone call or meeting. An unacceptable outcome might be "build the relationship" or the client saying, "I'll call you." An outcome like build the relationship is a worthy goal, but it's not defined clearly enough. An acceptable outcome might be "I want you to meet with the president on Thursday or Friday of next week" or "I want you to meet with the head of planning when she comes to town on April 4th."

During every marketing meeting with a client, you want to know when you've achieved success. The only problem is that most professionals aren't hired based on one meeting. In fact, it might take dozens of meetings and several years. In that case, what can you do? Wouldn't it be nice if you could score yourself after each and every marketing meeting? Well, you can, and here's how: You get an advance. The term advance was first introduced by Neil Rackham in his best-selling book *SPIN Selling*. I have modified Rackham's definition so it applies to professionals. An advance has three elements: (1) a commitment (2) to take action (3) in a definite time frame. If any one of these elements is missing, you have not secured an advance. If your meeting ends with an advance, you've made measurable forward progress in building the relationship.

During my workshops, I'll frequently ask participants whether they follow the game of cricket. Not surprisingly, with most U.S. and Canadian audiences, this draws blank stares. After feigning mock surprise, I ask why such disinterest. Most audiences say they don't understand the game, it's not part of their culture, they don't know how to keep score, and they don't know the rules of the game. I then point out that it's the same thing with marketing. What the concept of an advance offers is a very tangible way to keep score in any given marketing meeting. Get an advance and you score a point. All too often, professionals have no idea what just happened in a given meeting or they presume, incorrectly, that they have failed. For the first time in their professional lives, they can learn to keep score from minute to minute.

If there were a "practicality meter" that could somehow measure the usefulness of concepts delivered in a training session, this one idea would "peg the meter" on usefulness.

Most professionals make one of two common mistakes. They head off to a marketing meeting without having written out (or thought of) a single advance. Or they go to the other extreme and ask for work prematurely when no need is evident. The rainmakers head into meetings with multiple arrows in their quivers. They usually have thought of several advances. The best among these get the client to suggest an advance or they tell the prospect what they'd propose to happen next.

If you neglect to write down these three things when preparing for your next meeting, you will, in my opinion, be having a Random Act of Lunch.

WHAT SHOULD I DO IF I DON'T GET AN ADVANCE?

Getting an advance sounds simple, but it's very hard to learn at a skill level. In fact, it's far more likely that you won't get one. The following are clearly not advances because they are missing one or more of the three elements. They are also "conversation stoppers" for most professionals because as soon as we hear any of them we tend to end our inquiries. What the top producers in professional firms do with these statements is to ask more questions. They work diligently at seeing if the client will commit to an advance. The very act of trying to secure an advance gives you a better read on where you really stand.

Let's consider several client comments you might hear and how you might respond. Even though none of these statements is an advance, you will notice as we move down the list the comments are more and more encouraging.

"LET ME THINK ABOUT IT." Too many professionals automatically assume that every prospective client who says this is politely rejecting them. In a high percentage of situations this may be true, but not always. The client may genuinely need to think about something you discussed with him or her. Probe further by asking a question like, "We've covered a number of issues during our meeting. Is there anything in particular that stands out for you?" or "What portion of our discussion do you need to think about?" If the person says no to the first question, he or she is probably giving you the brushoff. Those who are genuinely interested in your services might start asking for more detail or clarification on something you discussed.

"I'LL CALL YOU." Again, many interpret this as a brushoff statement, but not your best marketers. To them it's an opportunity to secure a commitment. The more assertive rainmakers might say, "Great! When?" The less assertive ones might respond by offering to follow up if they don't hear from the prospective client in the near future: "If I don't hear from you within the next week or so, is it okay if I call you?" or "Would you like me to take the responsibility of getting back to you if I don't hear from you in 10 days?" One of the humbling discoveries made by my clients is that they are used by prospective clients as human "daytimers." To some that lesson comes as a terrible shock. If you don't possess enough humility to accept this reality, you are not going to reach your full marketing potential. To the rainmakers, it comes with the territory. Those who are the most insecure have the hardest time when someone doesn't call as promised or won't return their calls. Get over it. It often turns out these same people are very bad at returning others' calls.

"LET ME TALK WITH THE PRESIDENT (OR SOME OTHER DECISION MAKER)." Some professionals immediately suggest that they meet with the president as well. That approach may work in a small percentage of cases. However, in most cases you'll be moving too fast. You'll be diminishing the importance of your contact, and it could be interpreted as going over his head. If you inquire further, you may find out all kinds of useful information, such as how often your contact meets with the president and whether this issue will be discussed. Ask a question like: "When might you speak with the president about this issue?" An even better response is: "What do you think her reactions will be to our discussion?" or "How do you think the president will react to these ideas?"

"I LOOK FORWARD TO WORKING WITH YOU." A response used frequently is "I look forward to working with you too." Most professionals will happily stop there. Rainmakers, after expressing their mutual desire to work together, would ask questions like "What do you think the next step ought to be?" or "Where do we go from here?"

"WE WILL SEND YOU THE NEXT MATTER WE GET." Work to find out how many of those matters or projects the client receives each month. If they only have one per year and they just got one in and gave it to a competitor, you're in for a long wait. If they receive one per week and you don't hear from them for three months, that's telling you something else altogether.

It would be impossible to list all the possible comments that clients make that fall short of an advance. The important thing is to see whether you can turn these vague commitments into an advance.

If you become skilled at finding needs,
the client will ask for the business.

┌─────┐
│ 18 │
└─────┘

THE MYTH OF ASKING
FOR THE BUSINESS

Do I Have to Ask For the Business Right Away?

Many professionals privately confess that they don't know how to ask for the business. This is a constant complaint and why rainmakers are so highly valued. Yet there are very few marketing skills as misunderstood as knowing how to ask for the business. Some professionals are better at it than they realize, while others are much worse.

For professionals who hate asking for the business, I've got good news—you don't have to do it. At least not the way you might think. The most common misconception about asking for the business is thinking you must ask for work in an initial meeting or early in the relationship-building stage. Many younger partners (and sadly many older partners) are visibly relieved when I urge them not to do this. It is almost always inappropriate to ask for work during a first or second meeting. If a relationship needs months or years to develop, don't rush it. It's the equivalent of walking up to a total stranger and asking if he or she would like to marry you. This all-at-once approach almost always meets with rejection. I've heard more than one client say he will never hire a particular professional because he was turned off by that person's aggressive approach. If all professionals were on the receiving end of such marketing approaches, they'd quickly realize that the most effective course focuses on continuing the relationship in some tangible way rather than asking for the business.

You may wonder, "If that's so, why do some professionals passionately swear by this method?" They have very thick skin and sometimes it works! Not very often, but more often than never asking at all. It just doesn't feel very comfortable to most of us. The net result is that you will experience more rejection, and none of us likes rejection.

Suppose you're meeting with the CFO of a large company and she says she's "not happy with" her banker. What should you do? The really audacious professionals don't even ask why the unhappiness exists; they just ask for the business. Consider the feelings of this corporate officer who has just told you she's not happy with her banker. She is probably frustrated and possibly even embarrassed. It's a reluctant confession. Contrast that with the typical thought of the banker who hears such a statement, "Hooray, this is a live opportunity!" This results in a serious disconnect between the two. It may seem counterintuitive, but the most powerful way to develop trust with this kind of client is to help her resurrect the relationship with her current banker. That's right! Don't try to take advantage of the situation. The more respectful you are about the existing relationship, the more the client is attracted to working with you—eventually.

Fortunately, most professional service providers don't ask for the business, but instead have the common sense and decency to ask why the client is unhappy. Where many professionals are tripped up is what they say after hearing the client's answer. Suppose the client says, "My professionals aren't responsive." Inexperienced marketers will jump all over this comment as a chance to tell the client how responsive they are. This is not the time to make a sales pitch. Amazingly, there are many professionals who equate a sales pitch with asking for the business. They are *not* the same. Seeing professionals approach the situation in this way is embarrassing to watch.

Statements such as "Send us a file," "Send us a project," or "Give us a chance" are often tried. Most of the time they fail. These statements may work with a long-time friend or someone for whom you've done work in the past, but people who barely know you will interpret these comments as pushy and unhelpful. I'm not sure your friends will like it either.

Never ask for the business before you have developed sufficient trust with the prospective client. You earn trust through your behavior. I would suggest you keep asking questions until you get to the root of the client's concern. In the situation mentioned earlier, an appropriate question might be: "Can you give me an example of the firm's lack of responsiveness?" The reason I suggest you ask for examples is that you will gain insight into what this client considers responsive. As "responsive" is open to many interpretations, you'll want to know specifically what she expects.

Keep asking questions until a feeling is divulged or is easily inferred. Suppose the client says, "My lawyer promised me his summary of cases by Tuesday at 4 p.m., but didn't get them to me until 9 the next morning." If you ask a question such as "How did the missed deadline affect you personally?" you might hear, "I went into the executive committee meeting that evening without the information I needed and it looked as if I didn't know what I was doing." Translation: "I was embarrassed." A follow-up question you might ask is: "Is this the first time this has happened?" If the answer is yes, do what you can to help the client resurrect the relationship. If the answer is no, you might ask, "Are you at a point where you are ready to switch counsel?"

The best rainmakers, sometimes without even knowing it, get the client to suggest the next step. In other words, the client asks for the business, rather than you. Nevertheless, there are two questions you should make a regular part of your meeting ending repertoire: "What do you think the next step should be?" and "Where do we go from here?" Either one gives the client a chance to define how you should move the relationship forward. If you end more marketing meetings with either of these two questions, your effectiveness in asking for the business will skyrocket.

These two questions are not a panacea. One of the worst things you can do is to ask for the business well before you have developed sufficient trust with the prospective client. Follow the guidelines set forth above and you will definitely improve your rainmaking.

You will reduce the number of objections that arise if you culti-
vate an attitude of wanting to be of immediate help to a
prospective client.

19

DEALING WITH OBJECTIONS

How Do I Handle a Client's Objections?

Many sales training courses promote the belief that handling objections is a valuable skill. I disagree. In my opinion, the more valuable skill is preventing them! Great rainmakers are usually masters at preventing objections rather than overcoming them. If that's true, how do you prevent objections? Simple. Listen very carefully to what the prospective client is telling you. Your desire to understand the client must outweigh your desire to make the sale. Too often we make the sale more important than the relationship. It's the other way around.

You have more control over keeping objections at bay than you may think. The "magic bullet" is called preparation. If you prepare thoroughly, you won't hear as many objections. Preparation requires you to consider the personal needs and fears of the prospective client and prepare the questions you intend to ask. Many of us are so driven by what *we* need that we simply do not hear what the *client* needs. You will reduce the number of objections that arise if you cultivate an attitude of wanting to be of immediate help to a prospective client.

If you always seem to be bombarded with objections, you are probably making the classic selling error of telling more than asking. This is where most professionals fall down. Most objections are evidence of poor listening, lack of rapport, and sloppy selling practices. You can't endlessly talk your way past objections. Some professional service providers, such as lawyers, can be brilliant advocates. Yet that strength can quickly turn into a weakness if they treat client objections as a chance to flex their adversarial muscles. Treat every objection as a call for deeper understanding and you'll move past them with greater ease.

Sometimes, no matter how well you listen, objections will surface. When they do, follow this three-step method for handling them effectively. I first learned of this method from my friend, Jim Meiggs, who was formerly the marketing director of a Big Five accounting firm.

1. ACKNOWLEDGE THAT YOU HEARD AND UNDERSTOOD THE OBJECTION. Doing anything less tends to make clients become very belligerent. This step shows you understand the client's point of view. Never argue with the client because doing so only increases opposition and alienation. Alienation is not a great marketing tool. Warning: Some professionals in more contentious specialties are so used to confrontation that they often argue even when they think they're not. If you don't believe me, ask your spouse.

2. AGREE WITH AS MUCH OF THE OBJECTION AS POSSIBLE. If there is merit to part of it, there is no sense dancing around that fact. You'll end up looking foolish or evasive and it will destroy any trust built to that point. Suppose the client says, "I want to hire you, not some junior associate." You might respond this way: "It's true that you will be working with my trusted associate more often than with me. That's to hold down fees without compromising quality. You'll find Chris does a great job and knows your industry inside and out."

3. DESCRIBE HOW YOUR PROPOSAL HAS GREATER VALUE THAN DOING NOTHING OR YOUR COMPETITOR'S OFFERING. Face the fact that you always have competition; it's called the status quo. This step can't be done without a deep understanding of what the prospective client needs.

There is another technique you can use when faced with objections. When you hear one, reframe it in your mind into the form of a question. A shift in your attitude is required in order to make this work. Consider the frequent objection many professionals dread hearing: "You're too expensive." The client may be saying "buzz off" or could be saying "I can't sell it or justify it internally."

You can reframe the statement in your own mind to any of these questions: "How can I justify your fees to others in my company?" or "How can I justify your fees to my boss without looking foolish?" or "How can I sell your hourly rate internally given that it's 50 percent higher than our other outside advisor's rate?" Coming back with an answer to the client's question, instead of getting into an argument over the client's objection, puts you in a less adversarial mindset. For example, "While my hourly rate is higher than that of other firms, you'll find that I spend half the hours. This leads to lower fees on the project."

Even the best rainmakers don't win them all. Don't torment yourself if the prospective client remains unpersuaded. Even though our egos like to win every time, we don't have to overcome every objection. If you handle them poorly, you'll do irreparable harm to the relationship. The top producers want the relationship to outlive the objection. After all, objections are temporary. Ideally, the relationship is forever.

When it comes to winning over clients, don't tell them what you can do for them; demonstrate it.

$$\boxed{\textbf{20}}$$

WHY CLIENTS HIRE YOU

WHAT ARE THE DECIDING FACTORS THAT CAUSE
CLIENTS TO HIRE ME?

In an earlier chapter, I laid out a three-step process you can use to prepare for your marketing meetings. In this chapter, I will elaborate further on the first step: *considering personal needs*. Most professionals give superficial thought to client needs, when they think about it at all. Most fail to consider the important distinction between personal needs and organizational needs. That is a mistake.

Organizational needs don't prompt clients to hire you in the same way as personal needs do. Consider the client who is hiring an accountant, or any other professional for that matter. If you asked a group of accountants to list a client's personal needs, they might say something like "keeping fees down." In fact, that is an organizational need, not a personal one. If you probed further and asked that same group what personal needs derive from that organizational need, you might hear something like "stay within my budget" or "increase my bonus compensation" or even "look good to my boss." That does not mean your client would acknowledge any of these personal needs to you. You'll know you're dealing with personal needs when the client uses trigger words such as "I," "my," or "mine."

As you might imagine, the kinds of personal needs that might influence a client's decision to hire you are almost infinite in number. The number of personal needs that are deciding factors, however, shrinks that number radically. It's uncanny how often the same personal needs keep popping up as deciding factors. The list of personal needs that are deciding factors are things such as control, power, feeling understood, save time, know my industry, look good to my boss, work with female professionals, have fun, respect, reassurance, staying under budget, maximizing bonus compensation, chemistry/rapport, avoid surprises. Now be honest—would you have written down these kinds of personal needs on your piece of paper prior to a marketing meeting? I'll bet not. You'll save lots of time while preparing for your next marketing meeting by consulting this list as a starting point.

Most personal needs are left unspoken and unwritten. I contend that this list is mostly common sense, but given the number of professionals I coach who ignore these needs, I'm not so sure. Let's consider some of them:

"Give Me Control"

Control is almost always a factor and can ruin more sales chances for professionals than any other single factor if ignored (or if you're oblivious to it). If the buyer of your services has a considerable need for control during the buying process and he or she interacts with a professional who also has a need for control, watch out. The need for control can manifest itself in many ways. For example, some clients want to be consulted on every development, no matter how large or small. Others want you to consult them only on major milestones in your work. Ignore the client's need for control at your peril.

Control issues come up frequently during my workshops in the ways people attempt to secure an advance. There is a considerable difference in effectiveness between the professional who says, "I'll call you in two weeks" and the one who is more aware that control is a factor and says, "Is it okay with you if I call in two weeks?" The difference is subtle, but significant for the client who has the need for control in the buying process. The professional who insists on keeping control of the selling process will experience lots of frustration while marketing.

"I Want to Feel Understood"

Feeling understood is a nearly universal human need, whether you're in a selling situation or not. The best way to demonstrate understanding is to be a great listener. And the best way to stay disciplined about listening more than talking is to ask questions. This is in part why I insist that you write out your questions before you head off to a marketing meeting. Even if you've heard the client's story a hundred times before and you know exactly how to help him or her, you must have enough discipline to keep asking questions you already know the answer to so the client's need for feeling understood is met.

"Help Me Get a Promotion"

Power is another universal human need. It can manifest itself in a variety of ways, but the most frequent way professionals see it is in clients who are intent on "increasing the size of my budget" or "moving up the career ladder."

"Working with Female Professionals"

There is a growing female network within the business world. Be alert to female executives who want to work with female outside service professionals. If you are male and meet with one of these executives, you have to be willing to recognize when you can't meet that need. Instead, introduce these people to the female partners in your firm.

"Have Fun"

All else being equal, many clients will make fun the deciding factor. Remember from our earlier discussion the professional who asked two of her clients why she was hired? In both cases their answer was that she was fun to work with.

"Make My Life Easier"

Most professionals are oblivious to the fact that their in-house contacts likely deal with many other professionals from different firms so they have a basis for comparison that the outside professionals do not. You may think you are very responsive, but you may not be when measured against other outside professionals. On a comparative basis, you may end up in the middle of the pack or worse. To avoid this, start asking these questions of your current clients:

1. "How does the value we provide compare to what other firms are doing?"

2. "How can we become even easier to do business with?"

3. "Who is your best outside service provider and what can we learn from him or her?"

Clients are continually making judgment calls about how easy you are to deal with, and if you're viewed as "high maintenance" you won't be getting more work. As one client griped, "Sometimes I have to spend time managing both the problem and my outside professionals." That's bad because it makes you high maintenance and very expendable. Those outside professionals who are easiest to work with get the most work. Being sensitive to all the needs of your clients is essential to being able to serve your clients effectively. A professional from the Midwest received a phone call from a senior officer of one of his clients. She called to let him know she would not be getting back to him during the upcoming week since she would be on vacation. He could sense panic in her voice, so he asked her if she'd like him to field phone calls for her while she was away. She gratefully accepted his offer and thanked him for offering to help. As it turned out, he fielded four or five questions while she was away. This was added work that the professional would not have had otherwise, and the goodwill he gained from doing so was priceless. It also offered him a change of pace on the kinds of questions he was usually asked by this client. A less enlightened professional might have thought the client was simply buying professional services, but the client was really buying something much more valuable—a worry-free vacation.

"BECOME INTIMATELY FAMILIAR WITH MY BUSINESS"

Clients want you to learn about their industry and business before you are hired, not after. Sophisticated buyers of professional services will rarely hire you if you fail to make the up-front investment in their businesses. Once you're hired, offer to send your junior people to visit the client's premises (off the clock) to learn more about the client's business. Another way to "invest" is to set up proprietary websites (called extranets) that are custom designed with the client's business in mind. A useful extranet that makes needed information accessible to clients 24 hours a day, seven days a week can lead to increased profitability. Trademark matters and complex lawsuits are just two examples where this approach can be very effective. In one case, general counsel loved his products liability trial lawyers because they were all able to recite company part numbers with ease. Very impressive and devilishly hard for competitors to duplicate. Or try this novel approach: Buy stock in the company you are courting. Such actions send a very favorable message.

Another reason clients want experienced professionals who know the industry is that they can be deployed to give junior executives some seasoning and support. The deal may not happen if junior executives are left to their own devices. A senior professional with intimate knowledge of the industry can keep deals from collapsing due to inexperience.

One rainmaker attended the grand opening of a new grocery store operated by her client at seven o'clock one morning. It involved a new grocery store concept that her client was very excited about. During the visit she made a point of saying hello to the president of the grocery chain. When she got to the office she went to her associate and asked, "What do you think?" Her associate responded, "What do I think about what?" She said, "The store that opened today just two blocks from your house. What did you think of it?" The associate replied sheepishly, "I was planning to stop by this afternoon." His mentor said, "Go now! Don't wait!" This is a powerful story for many reasons, not the least of which is the genuine message of caring it sent to this client. The associate learned a valuable lesson: Make it your business to know when your client has a significant business event such as a grand opening of a new store. Know when the store first opens and make a point of going there first thing on your way to work. Waiting until later in the day would have wiped out her chance to say hello to the president. Investing 10 minutes on the store visit allowed her to demonstrate to the client that she cared.

"DELIVER FAR MORE VALUE THAN YOUR COMPETITORS"

Client representatives will spend no time reviewing bills received from trusted outside advisors. In other cases where little value is delivered, expect the fine-tooth comb. Here are just a few of the silly billing mistakes reported to me by clients. One client received a bill from her outside professionals that included her interview phone call and drafting of the engagement letter. In another case, the client was billed by an outside professional for the time he spent working up the bill! Another professional billed his client for the cab driver to wait the two hours it took him to perform a task for his client. One general counsel was billed for running a conflicts check! The list continues ad nauseam.

There is a lot of talk about alternative billing, but hardly a firm is offering it. Your clients want you and your firm to have some "skin in the game," which is why alternative fees have such appeal. You should be paid a premium for better than expected results and less when the outcomes aren't favorable to your client. To learn more about what clients value, here are two questions you might ask your existing clients:

- "What alternative fee arrangements do you have with other firms that you'd like to explore with us?"

- "What's the most attractive billing arrangement you've heard about between an outside professional service firm and its client?"

"DON'T SELL ME ANYTHING; HELP ME SOLVE MY PROBLEMS"

A senior executive at Owens Corning was quoted in a recent business magazine[1] as saying, "What is important in the long run is for suppliers to spend less time selling themselves and more time thinking about how to solve Owens Corning's problems." The problems don't have to be big ones. One simple solution to a recurring client problem is to have a professional fill in temporarily for the in-house professional who is out on maternity leave.

You are vulnerable if you are not saving your client money or increasing its profitability. Debra Snider, former executive vice president, general counsel, and chief administrative officer with Heller Financial, asked her outside professionals to go one radical step further: Turn the legal department into a profit center! With the eventual cooperation (via something called partnering) from her outside professionals, that's exactly what she did. For more on how she did it see the Autumn 2000 issue of *Law Firm Governance*, published by Aspen Law & Business.

"HELP MY BUSINESS SUCCEED"

It helps to realize that what you're selling to your business clients is not strictly professional advice, but actually advice on how to make their businesses more successful, even if that involves issues within your specialty as a professional. A Midwest patent lawyer, with prompting from his coach, decided to call his old college roommate, who owned a company in his city that manufactured products for others. One of the action steps he hoped to achieve during the call was to secure his roommate's agreement to give him a tour of the plant. The call went well and his roommate was delighted to give him a tour. In a debriefing with his coach after the tour, this patent lawyer said it felt "awkward" talking about business with his old roommate. Nevertheless, when asked how the tour went, he reported a sense that they were operating without patent protections. His ever-supportive coach said, "So what?" This particular company sometimes ends up enhancing the products it makes for customers. So if someone at the company comes up with a great manufacturing solution and the company doesn't patent it, one of the employees could walk out the door and turn it into a competing business. Something similar had happened to them with a wiper blade customer. That change is now in the public domain, which means they can't profit from their innovation.

The coach then asked if his friend understood the upside of operating with patent protections. Further discussion with this lawyer led to the realization that if this company patented its process it could license the process back to its customer or sell it to the customer and charge a premium. This patent lawyer was asked what he was "selling" to his college buddy. His response was, "My patent expertise." After further probing, he realized that what he was selling was a potential new revenue stream or an increased profit margin. Either way he was selling business advice. The light bulb went on. He was much more enthusiastic about going back to his college roommate to talk about how to help him make more money!

"Avoid Surprises"

Treat surprises the same way as you'd treat dead fish. Don't keep them around very long, because the longer they sit there the more they smell. Unlike the previous factors listed, this one is more likely to get you fired, not hired. Professionals systematically send out surprises to their clients every month in the form of invoices. When you send out a surprise bill, it could wreak havoc on other personal needs, such as "staying under budget" and "looking good to my boss." Pick up the phone and call the client to tell her the exact amount of the bill and offer to meet with her to explain why it got that way.

In another situation, the general counsel of a telecom company was heading from New York City to Washington, D.C., on the train when he opened up *The New York Times* to find out his company had been hit with a large judgment. Needless to say, he wasn't happy with this surprise and loss of control, and ended up firing his outside firm.

Technical Skills

Sometimes, technical skills are cited as a personal need, but technical skills are rarely a deciding factor. Technical brilliance is highly overrated by most professionals. The truth is that technical brilliance is merely the ante you need to get in the game. Most clients won't even consider you if you don't pass a threshold test of competence. In some cases, an overt display of your technical prowess can even be a liability. For example, the general counsel at one company said she goes ballistic when she asks her outside lawyer a question and gets a brilliantly researched and written 30-page memo in response. Her original (and unstated) purpose for asking the question was to save time. Thirty-page memos aren't time savers. A phone call to discuss the answer would have been preferable. General counsel hire outside attorneys for solutions, not for memos.

Outside professionals need to emphasize speed over quality. I am not saying that quality doesn't matter, because it does. It's just not going to be the differentiating factor in being hired. When there is a clash between speed and technical perfection, speed will almost always be the differentiator. Too many in the professions reach the opposite conclusion. Writing a "publishable article" for clients who are very busy shows brazen insensitivity to their needs. One lawyer wrote several letters to general counsel replete with cases cited in all the detail required by the Supreme Court. It drove his client nuts. Finally, he was warned never to do this again! If you are in-house and work with professionals who don't get it, send this chapter to them; maybe they'll get the hint.

What clients need and expect from their outside professionals can vary widely, so make sure you ask plenty of questions before, during, and after the engagement commences to divine what they want. There are many personal needs that are left unspoken, but universally cherished by clients. If every member of your professional team were focused on these personal needs, you'd never lose any prized clients. What this boils down to is increasing your empathy for others. If you continually strive to see the world from the client's perspective, you will be very good at catering to his or her personal needs, and your best rainmaking days will be ahead of you.

To improve your odds of success when cross-selling, prepare for your next meeting with a partner as if you were preparing for a meeting with a prospective client.

21

MAKING CROSS-SELLING WORK IN YOUR FIRM

How Do I Approach My Partner About a Cross-Selling Opportunity?

Leaders from nearly every firm I work with express a strong desire to improve their firm's cross-selling. Think of cross-selling as introducing your partners to clients, or vice versa. Most firms and professionals do very poorly at this vital firm function. Why the dissonance? Some of it may be due to poorly designed compensation systems, but too often that's used as a scapegoat. I've seen too many instances of effective cross-selling occurring in firms with an "eat-what-you-kill" culture to conclude that compensation systems are the chief culprit. Even if cross-selling as a firm-wide practice doesn't catch on, there are dozens of things you can do to improve in this area. Let's consider six.

Convey Your Passion for Your Work

Regardless of the compensation system, your passion for your work can be a great catalyst for cross-selling. For example, during a coaching meeting with two professionals from the same firm, I asked them each two questions: "What do you do?" and "What do you love most about your practice?"

Their answers to the first question were perfunctory, but the employment specialist's impassioned answer to the question about what she loved most triggered an immediate reaction from the other professional. The latter realized that one problem he had been dealing with was an opportunity to introduce his partner to his client. He also volunteered that until that moment he had been viewing the employment issues as problems to solve, rather than as an opportunity to introduce the client to his partner. Situations like this abound in most firms.

Eliminate Your Entitlement Mindset

A surprisingly large percentage of professionals whom I coach approach cross-selling as an entitlement. The mindset is: "He's my partner; therefore he should make an effort to help me." This attitude is simply unrealistic. One professional referred work outside her discipline to a competing firm because she'd been burned by her own partner. That is done every day because professionals are afraid of making an introduction that reflects poorly on them. They want to enhance their relationships with clients, not set them back a notch.

There are two questions you should get in the habit of asking yourself before asking a partner to introduce you to a client. The threshold question is: "How will this benefit our client?" Ironically, this question is rarely considered in any depth by the partner seeking an introduction, despite many protestations to the contrary. Another related question is: "How will this personally benefit my partner?" Many professionals are astonished at the cooperation they secure from their partners when they actively and consciously consider how their partners will benefit from making the introduction. Consider the favorable impression the client will have of the intellectual property trial lawyer from the example above for demonstrating concern for the client's business beyond the scope of the litigation.

A word of caution. Most professionals feel a very strong obligation to introduce their clients to the very best person in the practice area in which their client has a need. If your firm's practice area isn't one of the best, as judged by your partner, forget about an introduction. To find out your partner's assessment, you must ask. If you are an unknown quantity to your partner, you are well-positioned to influence his or her perception of your expertise, but it will take some work. This raises another thing that you can do to single-handedly improve cross-selling within your firm: *prepare*.

ALWAYS PREPARE

Approach the meeting with your partner the same way you would approach a meeting with a new client prospect. At a minimum, read your partner's biographical summary before approaching him or her. It demonstrates respect and makes a great impression. Remember to write out needs, questions, and advances. That's right; prepare for your meeting with your partner the same way you'd prepare for a meeting with a prospective client. Here are several advances you might work toward with your partner:

- Have your partner call her client by the end of the week to explore a three-way meeting

- Have your partner call her client by the end of the week to explore a three-way conference call

- Have your partner determine her client's satisfaction level with a current professional and report back to you by the end of the week.

I am struck by how unclear most professionals are about their objectives for a meeting with their own partners when cross-selling is on the agenda. Do you seek a three-way meeting, a phone call from your partner to her client, or simply information concerning the client's satisfaction level with its current services in your practice area? I have coached many professionals on how to approach their own partners, and it's the rainmakers who stand alone in thinking through their objectives for meetings with their partners. The plain truth is that, if you don't understand the selling process, then you are not likely to be very good at cross-selling either. If selling is algebra, cross-selling is calculus.

Consider the partner in a two-man firm who was frustrated by his partner's unrealized promise of having him named as panel counsel.[1] His partner had been panel counsel for an insurance company for several years and knew the regional claims manager (that is, the keeper of the list) very well. It turned out that this unlisted partner had never asked his partner whether he was comfortable in supporting his placement on the panel; he just assumed that he would. Nor had he ever made in-depth inquiries about what efforts his partner had made on his behalf. In two minutes we had worked out a question that he should have asked his partner months ago: "Are you comfortable in supporting my becoming a member of the panel?" If he answered "yes," he had several options for moving forward with his partner. If he answered "no," he was prepared to ask this follow-up question: "What skills must I possess in order for you to be completely comfortable in advocating that I be added to the panel?"

Make Your Partners Look Good

One way to do this is to help your partners fill gaps in knowledge about their clients. Most professionals do not know nearly as much about their clients' businesses as they should. Which means the client contact partner does not know as much about the client's business as she needs to know to do an effective job of cross-selling. Those professionals who always seem to have their partners making introductions for them are great at helping their partners fill that knowledge gap.

Consider the case of a professional in a large firm who is asked by his client about the firm's expertise in another area. Most professionals in this situation send out a generic letter with biographical materials on the applicable practice group. That's a lot of wasted effort.

This very situation was faced by a commercial trial lawyer in a large firm who was asked by her client about the firm's environmental law capabilities. The lawyer prepared a generic letter on the firm's environmental capabilities. Fortunately, she consulted her marketing director's opinion of this letter. The marketing director tore up the draft and went to one of the firm's environmental lawyers to discuss the particulars of this client's problem, getting his help in drafting a decision tree letter. The client loved the letter and told the trial lawyer to "Do what's in that letter." In all likelihood, the earlier version of that letter would have gone in the trash, and all hope of cross-selling would have been lost.

IT'S YOUR RELATIONSHIPS WITH PARTNERS THAT MATTER

There is a pervasive assumption circulating throughout professional service firms that cross-selling should happen between practice groups and departments. The reality in most firms, however, even those that don't have an "eat-what-you-kill" system, is that cross-selling happens in pairs. If one partner likes and respects a fellow partner and wants to help him or her, he will do so. In the absence of this bond, the chances of cross-selling are remote.

What can you do to create that kind of rapport? First, eliminate the most common form of ignorance found in professional firm cultures: not knowing what your partners do. Show an interest in your partners' practices by making it your business to know their ideal client profiles. Compare the response "My ideal client is the one who pays me" with "My ideal client is a public company between $5 million and $50 million that employs more than 50 people." It's much easier for someone to tick through a list of clients to see who might fit the latter criteria. The former criterion is useless. The first time you ask your partner about his or her ideal client, you are more likely to hear the first, not the second response. To get the latter kind of response, you'll have to ask the same question two or three times, because the sad fact is few of your partners will know what their ideal client looks like. Then actively consider which of your clients fits this profile. Be forewarned that your partner may reciprocate by asking about your ideal client. So be prepared with your answer.

A rarely used relationship builder is to attend one of your partner's public speaking engagements. If you think he or she might be nervous about having you in the audience, ask first.

If you are unable to attend or you are in a remote location, ask your partner to audiotape the presentation and send it to you.

BECOME COMPULSIVE ABOUT FOLLOW-THROUGH

Lack of follow-through is a key reason why more cross-selling isn't happening in your firm. In the many coaching sessions I conduct with partners throughout the world, it amazes me how frequently the person with the most to gain from cross-selling fails to follow through to see whether a partner did what was promised. For example, one West Coast professional had no contacts with a client he had targeted for marketing purposes. One of his partners had a contact within this target company and she agreed to make an introduction. He had to inquire of her several times before a meeting was arranged. She was not opposed to arranging the contact, but it was not one of her highest priorities. His persistence finally paid off when a meeting happened a month later.

Consider the earlier example of the employment expert and her partner. Cross-selling didn't occur until the employment expert was introduced to the client. In that case, it took the partner several more months of prompting before the meeting was ultimately arranged. It's not that she was unwilling to set up a meeting; it just wasn't very high on her list of priorities. In my experience, lack of follow-through is one of the most common reasons why cross-selling bogs down.

Effective coaching can dramatically enhance your partner's follow-through. Instead of asking your partner, "Did you speak to your client?" ask, "How did your conversation with your client go?" The former question comes off as "big brother," while the latter question presumes competence. Coach your partner on the kind of questions he or she might ask in your practice area that will reflect favorably on him or her.

Individually, none of these six actions is magic. Taken together, they can make almost anyone a dynamite cross-seller.

Effective training should change specific behaviors,
not just raise awareness.

$$\boxed{22}$$

MEASURING RETURN ON INVESTMENT
IN MARKETING TRAINING

How Do I Measure My Return on Investment?

Any time your firm undertakes marketing training, it is investing two key resources: professional time and money. Professional service firms frequently look only at their direct cash outlay and hardly ever consider their professionals' time investment. If you put a dozen professionals through a three-day (24 hours of classroom) training program and you assume the average billing rate is $250 per hour, your firm is investing up to $72,000 in lost billable time. Add to this figure the actual outlay for hiring a trainer and you've invested quite a sum.

What is your return on investment (ROI)? Most firms don't even try to measure it. The ones that do look solely to each professional's increased originations. The most enlightened professional service firm leaders, however, realize return cannot be measured solely in terms of revenue gains. Some extremely valuable behaviors are very difficult, if not impossible, to measure, such as the level of caring your professionals and staff extend toward your clients, or your staff's desire to serve others, or your clients' devotion to using your firm. Nevertheless, the list that follows will get you closer to measuring these intangibles than will revenues.

Using originations (that is, the amount of new business you bring in) as your benchmark has another serious limitation: the time delay between the training and the increase in fees. Desirable client work might take several months or several years to develop. The link between cause (training) and effect (increased fees) is too attenuated. There are many activities that are precursors to increased revenues that can be measured in the 30 to 60 days immediately following a training program. I wish more firms would pay scrupulous attention to the following measurements before and after the training. If they did, they would rarely opt for classroom-only programs. That's because coaching is vastly superior at delivering results. This has been proven true by companies in other industries that have empirically measured the return on investment in training.

If you're a solo practitioner, a practice group leader, or a professional service firm leader who wants to get more systematic about measuring your return on investment, here are some ways to do it:

MEASUREMENTS FOR MARKETING TO EXISTING CLIENTS

1. More client meetings where feedback is sought. (That is, where the primary purpose is to ask clients how you and your staff are doing.)

2. More routine status calls made to existing clients. (This type of activity gets put off when professionals are busy.)

3. More "stay in touch" phone calls to dormant clients. (This type of activity also gets put off when professionals are busy.)

4. More visits to clients' offices. Go back through last year's calendar to get an idea of how many times you

visited clients last year. Make an effort to double your client visits.

5. More articles sent or offers to provide "extra value" type summaries to clients.

6. More referrals generated from clients and others in your network.

7. Asking more business-oriented (big picture) questions during meetings and phone calls with existing clients.

8. More follow-up phone calls to clients to see how they applied your advice.

9. More closing dinners with clients after the deals are done.

MEASUREMENTS FOR MARKETING TO PROSPECTIVE CLIENTS

1. More phone calls to arrange marketing meetings.

2. More marketing meetings. (The sales-phobic professional who goes from none to two per month would be making modest yet tangible progress.)

3. More "stay in touch" phone calls to firm alumni (former associates) and friends.

4. Increased preparation time, measured in minutes, before business development meetings. Prepare a list of needs, questions and advances.

5. More professional visits to prospective client websites.

6. Talking less and listening more during meetings. (Expressed as a ratio.)

7. More "advances" achieved each month. Greater focus on interim results at the end of every meeting.

MEASUREMENTS TO GAUGE THE EFFECTIVENESS OF SPEAKING ENGAGEMENTS

1. More speaking engagements per year to audiences filled with prospective clients or referral sources, not competitors.

2. More phone calls (not letters!) inviting people to your talk.

3. More business cards collected from the audience after each talk.

4. More phone calls made to audience members within 72 hours after you've spoken.

MEASUREMENTS TO GAUGE YOUR CROSS-SELLING

1. More lunches with different partners each month. (I know of one professional who was eating lunch at his desk 20 times per month and having lunch with the same partner the other two days. He's now having two lunches per week with different partners.)

2. More partner bios read before these lunches.

3. A majority of each meeting with partners is spent on marketing-related issues, not social chit chat.

4. More meetings with prospective clients that include another professional from your firm.

5. More time spent (measured in minutes) preparing for each partner lunch.

6. More "advances" secured from your partners during lunch.

The above measurements are not exhaustive, but they give individual professionals and firms a starting point. I have watched countless professionals build greater confidence and momentum by focusing on these kinds of realistic measurements.

Dollar for dollar and minute for minute, the return on your investment in coaching will be much higher than on just classroom training alone. Most professionals will learn more from a five-minute coaching phone call than they will learn sitting in a classroom for several days. With less training and more coaching, your firm can enjoy a dramatic return on its investment of professional time and the firm's precious resources.

When your work load is reduced, get out of your office
to meet with more people.

$$\boxed{23}$$

MARKETING IN SLOW TIMES

What Do I Do When Things Slow Down?

Many professionals consider it a badge of shame when their practices slow down. The thinking goes something like this: "If I were really that good, things would never be this slow." That kind of thinking is evidence of an incredibly fragile ego. It's also the single greatest obstacle to your getting out there and doing something constructive during the slow times. It's hard to develop and renew relationships when you're feeling insecure. Unfortunately, many professionals go into hibernation. That's the worst thing you can do when times are slow. You must commit to meeting with more people, not fewer. Even if you're the Einstein of your field, you will starve if you don't make an effort to connect with people. The bright side is that you have much more time to devote to building relationships.

A slowdown can even be self-inflicted. Here are some self-limiting beliefs that I've heard uttered on many occasions: "Mondays are rough, no one wants to receive a marketing call on Monday" and "Fridays are bad because people are trying to get out of the office before the weekend." Another self-limiting belief circulating among sales-phobic professionals is "December is not a good month for marketing." If we accept all of these as true (subconsciously in some cases) and we assume there are roughly 240 business days available each year for marketing, we have just shrunk the available amount of time for marketing by half, to about 120 days. If you find yourself gravitating toward this kind of thinking, stop yourself! These beliefs are toxic and can actually cause your practice to slow down!

Slow times can arise because you are changing your practice area, or because of an economic downturn, or you could be starting a new office in another city. Regardless of the reasons for your practice slowing down, you can take greater control of your own destiny. Here are ten things you can do right now to jump-start your practice:

PAY EXTRA ATTENTION TO YOUR EXISTING CLIENTS

Losing clients from neglect is totally avoidable and all too common. Get in touch with your existing clients on a regular basis. This is a great practice, even when you're insanely busy, but it's particularly valuable when things have slowed down. Here are several ways to increase your one-on-one time with clients:

A. Go visit their offices across the street, even if you could easily conduct your business over the telephone. You don't have to do this every day, but there is no excuse for not doing it when things have slowed down and you have the time. An important subset of this is to tour the client's operation. It sends a powerful message about your commitment to the client.

B. Visit an out-of-town client whom you've never met (or rarely meet) in person. The offer to meet, by itself, is sure to be well-received. A professional from Tennessee visited her health care client and met several people who had recently joined the client's organization. She found the visit to be an outstanding relationship building opportunity.

C. Do a free workshop or seminar for your client on an

issue of concern to him or her. Doing a workshop on an issue that keeps your client awake at night is priceless.

D. Offer to write an article for a client's publication, such as an internal newsletter.

E. Attend an industry trade conference with your client. This can be another bonding opportunity.

RECONNECT WITH DORMANT CLIENTS

Just about every professional has a dormant client who is overdue for a phone call. If that includes you, call him today. If you're not sure how to start that call see Chapter 30, "Staying in Touch with Friends and Clients."

INCREASE YOUR INVESTMENT IN MARKETING

Too many firms decrease their investment in marketing when a slowdown comes. That will almost surely begin a death spiral. Even if your firm won't pay for it, you could attend a Dale Carnegie course or some other seminar. You could even hire your own marketing coach to help you jump-start your practice. Just be sure it's an investment with a reasonable likelihood of generating a return.

ASK FOR REFERRALS FROM YOUR MOST LOYAL CLIENTS

For more on how to do this see Chapter 12, entitled "Generating Endless Referrals."

SET ASIDE A BLOCK OF TIME EACH DAY FOR MARKETING

This means writing the time into your calendar. Professionals tend to create busywork when things are slow and work on tasks that are neither urgent nor important. This is very damaging to turning things around.

READ A BOOK OR SEVERAL ARTICLES ON MARKETING

For example, you can reread some or all of this book.

DUST OFF YOUR ROLODEX

Pull out your Rolodex and comb through it to see if there are any friends or firm alums who are overdue for a phone call. See if you can parlay each call into a meeting.

Set Measurable, Realistic, Weekly Goals

Make three phone calls per week in which your objective is to secure one-on-one meetings.

Meet with Your Partners

Cross-selling is a very quick way to jump-start your practice if approached thoughtfully. Your approach is to find out more about their practices and ask them for introductions. For more see Chapter 21, "Making Cross-Selling Work in Your Firm."

Do More Matchmaking

If you become a matchmaker for others, you'll have more reasons to pick up the phone. You might introduce your client to a potential customer, introduce a partner to a potential client, or introduce your friend to a potential customer. The permutations on this one activity are nearly endless.

If all you're going to do is engage in mindless busywork that doesn't involve reconnecting with clients, friends, and referrals sources, get out of your office altogether. At least that way you won't be deluding yourself into thinking you're working. Slowdowns can happen to the best of us. A slowdown is a test of your character. People with great character will simply do whatever it takes to overcome the adversity. The last thing they will do is head into hibernation. When work picks up again, they will be better for having had the experience. Professionals I've coached who have been through slowdowns are very motivated marketers. A slowdown is a highly underrated way of transforming your practice. Several rainmakers I've worked with became great marketers after being in a slowdown. A slowdown isn't a death sentence: It's a wake-up call to take action and grow!

NETWORKING
SKILLS

*Great rainmakers are great career advisors
to people in their networks.*

24

THE TEN MOST COMMON NETWORKING MISTAKES

WHERE DO MOST PEOPLE GO WRONG WITH NETWORKING?

I have observed and coached many professionals in social situations and I see them making the same mistakes repeatedly while networking. Here is my list of the ten most common networking mistakes professionals make:

1. APPROACHING NETWORKING WITH A "WIIFM" MINDSET. WIIFM means "What's in it for me?" Nothing brands you an amateur networker faster than this mindset. Instead, think about how you can help someone. It makes a lasting impression.

2. MAKING NO ATTEMPT TO RECOGNIZE A LEAD FOR THE PEOPLE IN YOUR NETWORK. Most professionals, when asked, cannot articulate their clients' ideal customers. What's worse is that they can't describe their own partners' ideal clients.

3. EXPECTING AN IMMEDIATE QUID PRO QUO. The mindset is, "I did this for you, so you owe me something in return." I'm not suggesting you become a doormat, but networking is

a long-term process. As Harvey Mackay, author of *Dig Your Well Before You're Thirsty*, would say, "Dig your well before you're thirsty."

4. FORGETTING TO THANK ATTEMPTED AND SUCCESSFUL REFERRALS. Most professionals say they do this, but I'd be shocked if more than 2 percent of the population do this on a consistent basis. Professionals, when left to their own devices, practice their trades, rather than saying thanks.

5. MAKING RECKLESS OR LOW QUALITY REFERRALS. Don't refer your client to another professional without following up to see if both parties were happy they were introduced. Low quality referrals are a reflection on you.

6. NOT TAKING INITIATIVE TO HELP PROMOTE OTHER PEO-PLE'S SERVICES. Have you ever written an unprompted letter to benefit someone in your network? If not, write one today.

7. NOT INVESTING TIME EVERY WEEK TO HELP OTHERS. This doesn't require that you spend more time networking; rather, it requires more of a shift in mindset. After finishing an article you thoroughly enjoyed, ask yourself: "Who else might enjoy this article?" Then send it to him or her.

8. THINKING SHORT-TERM. Too many professionals think they should only join groups that will bring business quickly. Forget that! Join the Harley Owners' Group if you love riding Harleys.

9. LETTING YOUR NETWORK FORM HAPHAZARDLY. One U.S. litigator who is a partner in a small litigation boutique is married to a British national. He is frequently asked if he knows any immigration lawyers. His answer has been "no." After some prompting, this lawyer is now developing a cross-referral arrangement with one or more immigration lawyers.

10. MAKING NO EFFORT AT HELPING PEOPLE MANAGE THEIR CAREERS. The best rainmakers in the service professions are often masters at placing people throughout their client universe. If you want to make a friend for life, just spend time with someone who is between jobs.

Spend as much time networking each day as you do brushing your teeth.

25

NETWORKING ISN'T SELLING

How Is networking different from selling?

Networking is a well-visited topic about which scores of books have been written, but very few are geared toward professionals, who face boundless opportunities for networking in a wide variety of settings.

Networking, however, is a misused and outworn term with many negative connotations, so let me define what I mean by networking. It is "putting people together for their mutual benefit." I define it that way so it can't be construed as a selfish exercise. Great networkers focus on how they will help others. Selfish or self-absorbed people will never be great networkers.

One of my Nashville-based clients told me that, until he learned my approach to networking, his notion of networking was doing the "Music City handshake," where someone comes up to you, says "Hi," and never makes eye contact with you or immediately starts peering over your shoulder looking for someone else. For those of you who might be thinking, "There must be a better way," read on.

Selling and networking are not synonymous terms. It's easy to see the difference at the preparation level. (Yes, I'd argue a networking meeting requires preparation.) Preparing for a selling meeting involves your writing down three things: needs, questions, and advances. (See Chapter 17, "Avoid Random Acts of Lunch.") By contrast, a networking meeting calls for you to put only two things in writing: needs and "high energy" questions. Advances don't need to be considered when networking. Networking meetings, when done with focus and preparation, are a precursor to sales opportunities. So the more networking meetings you engage in, the more selling opportunities will arise.

Networking involves a much larger universe of people than those you might consider prospective clients who are candidates for buying your services. The illustration below shows the difference between networking and selling.

The center circle is your universe of *current* clients. The next ring outside it is your universe of *prospective* clients. I include dormant clients in this ring. Most rainmakers have a large circle of prospective clients, while the sales-phobic professional has very few, if any.

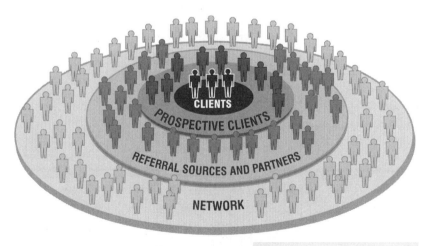

The Networking Circle

The third ring includes *referral sources* and *ideal client contacts*. A referral source is someone who has sent you work or is very likely to send you work. Satisfied clients and your partners would usually fall within this ring. Your ideal client is the person who actually hires you and usually (but not always) has the same title within an organization. If you're an accountant, perhaps it would be the CFO of a company. If you're an IT consultant, it might be the head of information technology; and if you're a lawyer, it might be the general counsel. Once again, most rainmakers have a large circle of referral sources and ideal client connections, while the typical professional has a dearth of these relationships.

The fourth ring encompasses your *network*. This includes neighbors, friends, the parents you meet at your child's sporting events, and virtually anyone else that you have some kind of relationship with. How you interact with the people in these rings will vary. The chapters in Part C of this book provide the best guidance for how to interact with prospective clients. The chapters on networking skills in this section are for people in the outer rings.

Ask high-energy questions if you want to take a conversation and the relationship to a deeper level.

$$\boxed{26}$$

WORKING FOR THE ROOM: NETWORKING DURING SOCIAL EVENTS

How Can I Work the Room in a Way That Leaves Me Feeling Comfortable?

Networking can be done in group settings and one-on-one meetings. In this chapter, we'll cover the dreaded exercise of working the room. When I am asked for advice on how to "work the room," I shudder. That's because it suggests something very distasteful. Instead of working the room, think of it as working *for* the room. These ideas are not meant to be the only means of making the most of social functions. They are meant to give you a structure for how to approach these common, everyday situations. Most professionals, when left to their own devices, will network without any clear purpose and waste lots of valuable time as a result.

First, let's consider some typical situations in which working the room might arise. You're going to the firm's retreat this weekend. You're about to go into a client's retirement party. You're about to walk into your firm's holiday reception. You're about to go into your firm's gala celebrating its 25th year of operation. You're about to walk into the networking portion of the conference you've been attending.

What immediately runs through your mind about each of these settings? Many people are intimidated by these situations—rooms full of people. Introverts are even more intimidated. I have worked with some very impressive rainmakers who openly bristle at the thought of walking into a room full of people. What can you do in all of these situations to increase your comfort level? I'd suggest you go into them with a purpose. Entering a room full of people with any one of these four purposes should increase your comfort level:

PUTTING OTHERS TOGETHER

Head into the room with the mindset that you are there to put people together for their mutual benefit. Remember the definition of networking set forth previously. Going into any situation by thinking about who you can help rather than who can help you puts you in a giving rather than taking mindset. Most of us warm up faster to people who are giving rather than taking. Most professionals see their comfort level skyrocket with this approach.

Here are three obvious ways to put people together:

1. Put a person who is in the room together with another person who is in the room. For example, during your firm's holiday party, you might introduce your best client to a prospective customer or supplier.

2. Put one of your partners together with a person who is in the room. For example, at your firm-sponsored function, you might introduce your client to your top-notch tax partner.

3. Put a person who is not in the room together with a person who is in the room. This one gives you the most flexibility because you are not limited to the people who happen to be in attendance. It also gives you a basis for having a conversation around it.

Entering a room full of strangers is certainly more intimidating than entering a room full of people you know. Putting a person who is not in the room together with a person who is in the room even works in a room full of strangers. High-energy conversations also work well in a room full of strangers.

ENGAGING IN "HIGH-ENERGY" CONVERSATIONS

Most of us dislike superficial conversation. Yet much of what passes for networking is superficial and lacking in depth. If you ask high-energy questions, you'll be far more likely to engage in high-energy conversations. If you don't like "high energy," think of it as memorable, lively, or enthusiastic conversation. Here are just a few high-energy questions designed to take the conversation and the relationship to a deeper level:

- "What do you love most about your work?"
- "How would I know if I were talking to someone who would be an ideal client for you?"
- "What's the most notable trend in your industry?"
- "How did you get started in this business?"
- "Which of your major competitors do you fear most?"
- "How do you tell the great [job title] from the good ones?"
- "What's the most exciting project you're involved with right now?"
- "How has the state of the economy affected your business?"
- "What is the most interesting book you have read in the past three months? What made it interesting?"

A high-energy conversation involves both of you talking about something that you are passionate or feel strongly about. It doesn't have to be a business conversation. While attending a networking function during a conference, one professional in private practice struck up a conversation with a prospective client whom she was meeting for the first time. She asked this high-energy question: "What do you love most about your work?" This didn't go very far because the prospective client hated his job. To her credit, this professional quickly shifted to a variation on the original question: "What do you love to do when you're not working?" This led to a passionate discussion about fly fishing. These two were eventually pulled apart, but the impact it made on the prospective client was lasting. He made a point of coming over to this professional at the end of the evening and said he enjoyed their conversation and would definitely be in touch.

The more interesting your conversation gets, the better, even if it is interrupted. In fact the interruption itself gives you an opening for continuing the discussion outside the networking event. One professional in Chicago had a fun discussion about the auto industry with a prospective client. They were pulled apart, but the professional realized he could comfortably call this person and suggest a meeting to finish the conversation. In another situation, a partner went to her firm's retreat and started multiple high-energy conversations that were interrupted and never finished. It hadn't occurred to her to call these partners up after the retreat to finish the conversations.

ACTING AS HOST RATHER THAN GUEST

Go into these settings with the mindset that you will act as a host rather than as a guest. A great host always tries to make his or her guests comfortable. So when starting a conversation with someone you've never met, ask a question that seeks common ground. If you can find common ground, it puts both of you more at ease. That's why a topic such as the weather is so widely discussed. Instead of discussing the weather, you might ask a question such as, "What is your relationship to the [host]?" If you're at a conference you might ask, "Is this your first conference?" or "Have you heard the keynote speaker before?"

This should facilitate your desire to match people up. Too often professionals show up at their own functions, retreats, or holiday receptions with a guest mindset. Your desire to ease others' discomfort will do wonders for easing your own. Upon entering the room, one rainmaker from Toronto makes a point of seeking out those people who are standing all by themselves and befriending them. You can make friends for life that way. This works particularly well in situations in which you don't know a single person in the room.

FINDING A SPECIFIC PERSON

Go into the meeting with the mission of finding a specific person. The person you're looking for may be a client you hope will be there that you don't see in person very often or it may be a client you've never met in person (only by phone) or someone you've always wanted to meet. You can then walk up to the first person in the room, even if he's a complete stranger, and ask, "Have you seen Charlene Gifford?" or "I'm looking for Charlene Gifford. Do you know what she looks like?" This has worked countless times for even the most introverted professionals. You can also use your "mission" as the reason for quickly excusing yourself: "If you'll excuse me, I'm going to continue to look for Charlene."

While I don't subscribe to the notion that you should collect as many business cards as possible during these functions, it's vital to collect business cards from those you meet for the first time and to whom you feel a strong connection.

MEASURING SUCCESS AFTER A GROUP EVENT

Here are some signs that your efforts were successful:

1. You make at least one calendar entry to do something for someone you met, then follow through on your commitment! (Note: If you make three entries after every event and do the follow-through, you will achieve rainmaker status in no time.)

2. You call someone whom you enjoyed meeting where the conversation was interrupted and suggest a meeting.

3. You engage in at least one high-energy conversation.

4. You make at least one introduction while at the event.

5. You find the person you are looking for.

There are many ways to approach networking, so you need not view the four purposes set forth above as exhaustive. If you don't like these four, devise your own, but devise one before you walk into the room. Following these suggestions beats standing around talking with your partners all night, which is what most people do when left to their own devices. Never show up without a purpose. Start applying these ideas and your networking can become more enjoyable. For some, I dare say, it will become fun.

When meeting with friends,
it's okay to talk about their business lives.

27

NETWORKING ONE-ON-ONE

How Do I Conduct Effective Networking Meetings?

More by default than intention, the most favored marketing activity of many professionals is the networking meeting. Most professionals approach these meetings either haphazardly or, worse, they equate them to selling meetings. When I use the term "meeting," I am referring to one-on-one meetings in any of these venues: breakfast, lunch, dinner, sporting events, and a host of other events too numerous to itemize.

In one year, the typical professional might spend hundreds of hours in meetings with friends. When I use the term "friends," this includes clients, dormant clients, former partners, college classmates, friends, neighbors, acquaintances, and referral sources. Time, by itself, doesn't guarantee that your networking meetings will deliver results. If your meetings (lunch being the most popular) consist of purely social discussions about the spouse, the kids, the dog, the golf game, etc., you are squandering precious marketing time. You might get work using this approach, but it's inefficient. Going about it this way is like standing on a street corner hoping that your future spouse bumps into you. It might happen, but it's very unlikely.

Some professionals go to extreme lengths to keep their personal and business lives separate. That is your choice. Often without consciously realizing it, some leap well beyond that and resolve never to talk business with their friends. They create a wall between what they consider acceptable and unacceptable topics of conversation. That is a mistake.

The real challenge when networking with friends is to convert a social discussion into a business discussion. Avoiding business discussions or allowing only superficial ones is a missed opportunity to deepen the relationship. Some professionals find it comforting to focus on learning more about how businesses work. Who is better suited to educate you on business issues than your friends? If you don't know much about what your clients and friends do during half their waking lives (work), then your relationship is shallow. Countless professionals feel a palpable sense of relief when I give them "permission" to discuss business with their friends.

Networking is best done with friends, not strangers. I work from the premise that your personal relationships are more precious than any work that might flow from the relationship. Read everything in this chapter through that filter.

What can you do before, during and after individual networking meetings where selling isn't comfortable or appropriate?

BEFORE YOU GO TO YOUR MEETING

1. DO YOUR HOMEWORK. Many professionals find it helpful to ask themselves before they pick up the phone: "Is there anyone I know whom this person might like to meet?" This approach is particularly effective with someone you don't know very well. The question almost always triggers a thought of someone. More importantly, it usually makes the caller more comfortable about picking up the phone because it takes him or her out of a "sales" mindset. Using this approach allows you to gear every phone call toward adding value.

Another variation on this approach is to ask yourself this question: "What have I learned recently that I can share with this person?"

2. PREPARE SOME QUESTIONS. Write down on a piece of paper three to four high-energy questions you might ask your friend before you go to your meeting. (See Chapter 26 on "Working FOR the Room" for such a list of questions.)

Some professionals worry about losing spontaneity if they prepare questions ahead of time. In truth, it has the opposite effect. Preparing questions makes you more spontaneous and flexible, not less. That's because you've given some thought about the person ahead of time.

Some professionals refuse to ask high-energy questions because it might trigger a negative reaction. I ask these skeptics, "For every person who reacts negatively, how many do you think will respond favorably to the question?" Usually the answer is, "hundreds." Then I ask whether it makes sense to avoid asking these questions altogether out of fear it might prompt a negative response in a small minority of cases. Clearly, that doesn't make sense.

DURING THE MEETING

1. LISTEN WHILE THE OTHER PERSON DOES MOST OF THE TALKING. No matter who you're meeting, I'll bet I know his or her favorite topic of conversation: himself or herself. It doesn't take a mind reader to figure that out. In fact, I've had several clients tell me they learned this from their mother before they went out on their first date. This is ancient wisdom.

If you don't listen more than you talk, you won't learn much. You can use this obvious realization to your advantage in all kinds of networking situations. We've all had the experience of letting someone else do 85 percent of the talking and then find out later that this person considers you a "great conversationalist." We talk about ourselves so much because most of us hunger to be understood. If you really want to turn people off, talk about yourself incessantly.

2. HELP THE PERSON REDUCE HIS OR HER "WORRY PILE." Assume every person you meet has a list of two to three top worries of the day. These could be either personal or business-related worries. These worries can and do change on a daily basis. The challenge is to build sufficient trust that your friend will share those worries with you. This requires fantastic listening skills. Your goal is to decrease his or her "top worries pile" during the meeting! Do this regularly and most people will jump at your offers to meet. If you insist on talking about number 17 on his or her list of worries, you won't get another meeting any time soon.

Suppose you show up for lunch with a friend, you've written out your list of high-energy questions, but it becomes obvious early in the conversation that this friend is looking to make a job change. Ditch your questions and do what you can to help the person brainstorm job opportunities.

The best rainmakers are masterful at placing people in new jobs. There is probably no better way to create friends and clients for life.

3. ASK FOR YOUR FRIEND'S OPINION OR ADVICE. Take whatever is on your worry pile to the meeting and ask your friend for advice on how to deal with it. This is the opposite of the previous idea. You can ask for advice on problem clients, problem employees, your career, how to handle fee disputes, and a host of other issues. This approach works well because it appeals to everyone's ego.

Asking your friends for advice on how to enhance your practice is a great way to enroll others in your success. An associate at a firm in Texas was interested in building his network and decided to meet a friend of his mother's who is the CEO of a local company. It was easy enough to get the meeting because this friend had suggested they get together. Being only a few years out of professional school, this person decided to ask for advice on how to build his practice. The plan went off without a hitch and he even secured his friend's permission during the meeting to call again if he had other questions on how to go about building his practice.

He followed up with this family friend a few weeks later after he tried his friend's suggestions to let her know how they worked.

This same approach could be used by associates who are looking to enroll a partner as a mentor. An associate could try this approach with three to four partners in the hopes that she'd end up with one partner who takes an active interest in her career.

4. ASK HIGH-ENERGY QUESTIONS. (See Chapter 26.) This approach is ideal for the professional who knows plenty of people, but isn't sure how to convert more of those contacts into business. When used inside your firm, these kinds of questions will promote more cross-selling. There is a tendency to think these questions won't work with long-time friends, but with experience I've found the opposite is true: It's where they work best.

Indeed, these questions are surprisingly effective with someone you've known for decades. An accountant from Minnesota asked her longtime friend and the chief financial officer of a Fortune 500 company how to tell a great CFO from a good one. This friend, who normally doesn't utter more than two sentences at a time, came alive and proceeded to bend his friend's ear with his answer for 15 high-energy minutes. My client was surprised and pleased with the response. What amazes me is how rarely professionals are willing to "risk" asking these questions of people they've known for quite some time. It's almost as if their relationships are stuck in a rut and they are afraid to move outside their comfort zones. Those who find the courage to ask are nearly always rewarded with new insights from long-time friends and clients. Most importantly, the relationship gets stronger.

None of these questions needs to be used verbatim. You can modify them to suit your unique situation. One of my clients didn't like the "Who is your ideal client?" question because he already knew the answer for his plumbing contractor client. Instead, we came up with these questions as a variation on the same theme: "What's the smallest project you like working on?" or "What's the largest project you can handle?" or "How has your competitor (a company that pre-installs plumbing) affected your business?"

Be sure to give a context for asking the question if you think it may be misinterpreted. For example, you could say, "May I ask you a crazy question?" or "I've known you for 20 years, but I'd be hard pressed to describe your ideal client" or "I'm curious about something."

5. ASK TRANSITION QUESTIONS. Transition questions allow you to bridge from a personal discussion to a business discussion without it feeling overly awkward. For example, if you have a friend who works for a company that just went through a merger, you could ask her, "How has the merger affected you personally?" This question is very personal and it gets you past the superficial very quickly. Or suppose your friend recently changed jobs from one company to another. You could ask, "How does working at your new company compare to working at your former company?"

Other transition questions that work well are, "What does your typical day look like?" or "What keeps you awake at night?"

6. LOOK FOR MUTUAL BENEFIT. Actively explore putting your friend together with someone for their mutual benefit. Remember, that is my definition of networking. One professional served on the board of the YWCA for many years. She had long wondered how to approach her fellow board member, Susan, who owns a direct mail company. As it turns out, this person knew two companies that were potential clients for Susan, so she proposed the idea of introducing them. Susan gratefully accepted the offer, and these two introductions were made. Needless to say, the relationship grew stronger. If you have a friend who already knows everybody, try helping his family members arrange job interviews or gain entrance to great colleges.

More clients are demanding that their professionals take an active role in helping their businesses succeed. Heller

Financial pays its outside law firms two basis points for referrals that are closed and funded. In calendar year 2000, Heller received 19 referrals from its outside firms and booked four deals worth $72,000,000.[1]

MEASURING PROGRESS AT THE END OF YOUR MEETING

One outcome that you can work toward is a meeting that ends with your friend saying, "We ought to do this again." This comment is an indication that you did a great job of focusing on his or her needs.

Another way to "measure" progress is when your friend says, "That's a good idea" or "I hadn't thought of that. I'll try it." In other words, deliver value during every meeting. Give ideas worth thousands of dollars away each time you meet.

Sometimes my clients report breakthroughs in their progress that are even more remedial. For example, they start discussing business-related topics halfway through lunch rather than waiting until the end of lunch. Or they start discussing business-related topics halfway through lunch rather than not at all.

There are an infinite number of ways to network effectively with friends. Doing any of the above tilts the playing field in your favor. Some professionals view this kind of networking as a "welcome break" from the demands of their practices. Great networkers do these things, and more, because they love doing them, not because they will lead to more business. The more thought you put into helping others, the more serendipity will happen. As you apply these ideas, your network will grow and you'll notice more opportunities finding you, rather than the other way around.

When telling people what you do, they will remember
your passion, not your job title.

28

YOUR ELEVATOR SPEECH

How Do I Respond When Asked "What Do You Do"?

Regardless of whether you find yourself in group settings or one-to-one meetings, you will always want to have your elevator speech ready to go. One of my clients, an appellate lawyer, said it's like preparing for the one question you know the court will ask you during oral argument. An elevator speech is a short statement of what you would say to your ideal client if he or she stepped on the elevator with you on the first floor and got off at the fifteenth floor. Ideally, the person hearing your response will feel your passion for what you do.

The need for an elevator speech comes up most often in social situations in which we are asked "So, tell me, what do you do?" Many professionals confess to hating this question. I ask this question of professionals in my workshops and coaching sessions. The responses I hear are often predictable, boring, and uninspiring. The worst response I've ever heard to this question is "I work in an office." How uninspiring!

Then I ask, "What is it you love most about your work?" Most people become much more animated, energetic, and enthusiastic when answering this question. The difference in their energy level between their answer to the first question and their answer to the second question is striking. I then challenge professionals forevermore to stop answering the first question. Instead, always reframe the first query as if you were asked the second question. Your answer to this second question is your elevator speech.

Answering the second question instead of the first provides several advantages in networking situations:

- Your answer is more memorable, which means *you* will be more memorable

- It differentiates you from others who do the same kind of work

- It draws people into the conversation at a deeper level

- Your answer is filled with more energy and enthusiasm

- It makes conversations more fun and less perfunctory

There is another practical reason for answering the second question. You'll get more of the work you most love doing. What are the chances that the universe will deliver to you the work you love if you don't tell people what you love to do? Don't keep it a secret!

It's really simple when you do the math. If only five people know that you love forensic accounting, you won't see much of that kind of work. If you tell another five people you meet at a single social function what you love, you've just doubled your chances of getting more of that work in one evening! Some professionals are wary about answering with what they love because they worry they'll be perceived by others too narrowly. In my experience, the reverse is true: the more narrow, focused, and passionate your answer, the more likely they are to ask if you do work in other areas. They connect with your passion for your work. My experience here illustrates the point. I tell prospective clients that I don't do classroom-only presentations, hence retreats aren't my area of focus. Nevertheless, I am asked frequently to conduct retreats. I agree only if the firm is willing to do them as a preview to a full program that includes my coaching.

This second question also doubles as a high-energy question. It works particularly well within a professional service firm. This means you can ask this question of the partners in your firm whom you don't know particularly well. Often there is an increase in the level of cross-selling once each partner learns more about what his or her partners love about their work. The sessions in which I've asked partners to pair up and ask each other the question nearly always generate new business opportunities.

Answering the first question is, in my opinion, networking without a purpose. Answering the second question is networking with a purpose. One corporate lawyer (who spoke fluent German) started answering the second question this way: "I am a corporate lawyer who represents German companies looking to do business in the U.S." His percentage of work representing German companies shot from 10 percent to 70 percent of his business in five years.

Other memorable responses to this question: A real estate professional who really loves doing one-of-a-kind transactions says he enjoys doing "wacko deals." A Chapter 11 bankruptcy lawyer refers to himself as a "corporate undertaker." There is no magic to your answer, but whatever it is, it must resonate from within. You can't fake an enthusiastic answer.

Do more with the network you have before worrying about growing a new one.

┌─────────┐
│   29   │
└─────────┘

DEVELOPING YOUR NETWORK

How Do I Develop My Network?

There is a myth circulating among professionals that "If I join the right groups, I'll magically generate a ton of business." For most of us, that's not true. Don't despair, however. Most of you don't need to join new groups because you already have plenty of relationships in your existing network. The real problem is that you don't do much with the network you already have. An example will illustrate this. A senior associate with a large firm started our coaching session by lamenting his lack of a network and his desire to build one. Three minutes into the meeting, I learned that he had been a professor at one of the local universities before going to law school. Turns out he had a list of the names of his former students—all 2,000 of them! Further probing revealed his belief that contacting his former students for marketing reasons was somehow unethical. When I asked him if he genuinely wanted to reconnect with his former students even if they never hired him, he said, "Absolutely!" I told him to go for it.

Which Group(s) Should You Join?

I am frequently asked which groups professionals should join for networking and marketing purposes. That's akin to asking me whom you should marry. That choice is a very personal one. Generally speaking, you should stay away from joining groups in which a majority of the members are your competitors. The exception to that is when you get a large percentage of your work through referrals from your competitors. My suggestion is to join only those groups you'd enjoy even if you never got an ounce of business from them. Therefore, if you love mountain biking, join a group of other mountain bikers. You're sure to have more fun and you are more likely to form lasting relationships.

Never join a group solely because you want to get more business. Don't join the chamber just because other professionals have had great success there. Join it because you really believe in its purpose and mission. We all know what happens if we join groups to which we feel no connection. We don't go to the meetings or, if we go, we show up late and leave early. Not many opportunities will surface with that kind of commitment. If you don't believe in the organization, you won't attend meetings regularly. If you don't go to the meetings regularly, you won't meet as many new people. Even when you do go, you won't have as much fun because you'll be unfamiliar with the issues and those who attend.

Is Your Network Underdeveloped?

Nevertheless, deciding which group(s) to join is a legitimate question for professionals in these situations, especially the first:

- Your network is underdeveloped. (You don't know many of your ideal clients.)
- You're relatively new to your professional practice.
- You are opening the firm's new office in another city.
- Most of your contacts have retired or are getting close.
- You are attempting to change your area of expertise.

To test how well-developed your network is, let's assume you are an employee benefits consultant who wants to step out from under the shadows of your more famous partner. Assume your ideal client is the CFO of a small or medium-sized company. The question you should be asking yourself is, "How many CFOs at small and medium-sized companies do I know who are not my clients?" If your answer is "dozens" or "hundreds," you probably don't need to join new groups. Instead, learn how to make the most of the relationships you already have.

Many professionals who are asked the above question have an underdeveloped network. Their answer is less than five ideal clients. It becomes immediately obvious where their networking energies ought to be focused. If you don't know many people in your target market, it can feel overwhelming to begin. Don't try to radically increase that number overnight. Instead, try moving the number from "two" to "four" or "three" to "six" within the next six months. Keep steadily adding to that number each year until your answer is "dozens" or "hundreds."

MEETING MORE PEOPLE

Once you join a group, how do you make the most of it? Regardless of the group you join, here are three proven ways to meet more people:

1. Become an active member of the speaker's committee.

2. Become active in the membership committee.

3. Earn a leadership position within the organization.

The first two committees are valuable precisely because your role in each is to seek out new people. You can call on high-profile businesspeople within your community who are total strangers and invite them to be speakers for your group. You won't be wearing your hat as a professional; you'll be wearing your hat as a member of the speaker's committee. The same holds true with the membership committee. You can call on every newcomer to your area wearing this hat. The higher the profile of your group, the more they're likely to be flattered by your request. These two committees can be used as a vehicle for increasing the size of your network by hundreds of people.

Taking a leadership position allows you to work alongside

your target audience. Through this quasi work relationship, they can assess your decision-making skills and expertise. Many professionals I've coached have met some of their best clients this way. Your shared passion for the purpose of the organization can be the perfect opportunity to build the relationship.

OTHER WAYS TO DEVELOP YOUR NETWORK

ENROLL YOUR SPOUSE IN THE EFFORT. You don't even have to join a group. Sometimes these opportunities appear right in your living room. The spouse of an advertising specialist in Portland was on the welcoming committee of a church group. As such, the couple would entertain new arrivals to their city every Friday in their living room! Fortuitously, many of these visitors were senior executives of prospective clients. During a coaching session, it dawned on the executive what an incredible opportunity this presented. He had never thought about these Friday evening visits as opportunities until I pointed it out to him. It seemed so obvious after the fact. This was his chance to be among their "first friends" in the city of Portland.

START YOUR OWN NETWORK. If there are no existing groups that have appeal, start your own network. An employment professional wanted to meet more human resource executives in her city so she started her own group and only permitted the top human resource executive from each company to attend the meetings. She was able to use the group as a platform for all kinds of interaction with her ideal target market. She became very well-known to all the top human resource executives in her city in less than two years.

USE SPEAKING AS A MEANS OF GROWING YOUR NETWORK. You can contact dozens of prospective clients in advance of your public speaking. (See Chapter 34.)

Adding people to your network takes time. But it won't seem like work if you're passionate about the groups you join. In fact, it will provide a sense of fulfillment. The key is to create a network that fits your personality and style. Life is too short to be meeting people who don't add value to your life.

The way some professionals resist calling friends and clients,
you'd think staying in touch required lifting
a 1,000-pound telephone.

┌─────────┐
│   30   │
└─────────┘

STAYING IN TOUCH WITH CLIENTS

HOW DO I GET BACK IN TOUCH WITH SOMEONE I HAVEN'T SPOKEN TO IN A LONG TIME?

Voice mail, e-mail, and other forms of technology can actually reduce our in-person connections with other people. As a result, I find an overwhelming majority of professionals hungering to reconnect with old friends and dormant clients, but they don't know how. Many are afraid their friends or clients will think they are only after work when being contacted after a long hiatus.

Most of us are uncomfortable about calling someone with whom we have totally lost touch. To be on the safe side before calling someone you haven't talked to in more than one year, examine your motives. If you are genuinely curious about how your friend or client is doing, make the call. If your primary motivation is to get more work, don't call. Ordinarily, when an old friend calls us out of the blue, we are not cynical; we're flattered.

One of the biggest barriers to professionals making these

calls is that they haven't thought about how to start the conversation. Once they have a clear idea about how they will begin, they almost always make the call. Your goal can be very straightforward: Arrange a meeting. If your friend lives in town, suggest a face-to-face meeting to reconnect—lunch, a drink after work, or whatever fits. If your contact doesn't live in your town, lay the foundation for a visit the next time you are in his or her city or see if the person has plans to be in your city. This step may seem obvious, but rarely do professionals remember to ask their friends or clients whether they have plans to be in their city during the coming months.

The amount of energy it takes to find a new phone number or e-mail address is enough to stop many professionals dead in their tracks. Enormous delays are incurred because professionals don't have this information. If this describes you, ask your secretary or assistant for help. One professional had been putting off a call to an old friend for more than a month for lack of the telephone number. Her secretary solved that mystery fast and she made the call the same day. You would be amazed at the number of people I coach who are frozen over such a tiny obstacle.

If you are looking for ways to reconnect with someone after a long hiatus, here are seven ideas that are time-tested and have proven to be effective:

1. CALL YOUR FRIEND (THE ONE YOU ARE THINKING OF RIGHT NOW). Start the conversation by saying, "I was thinking about you and wondered how you're doing." Then you have to do something really hard—shut up! Let your friend answer; don't rush to fill the silence. Nearly everyone who receives this kind of call will be flattered. Make three calls like this each week and you'll be among the best networkers in the profession. My personal practice is to pick up the phone immediately if I find myself thinking about someone two or more times in the space of several days. It works very well for me. During these calls, many people have commented that I must be psychic. Hardly. I'm simply honoring an internal prompt that everyone gets but most ignore.

An architect in Texas agonized over calling a client whom he hadn't talked to in over a year. He dreaded making the call, but after about a month, with prompting from his coach, he did so. To his delight, the call was well-received. During the call, this architect invited the client to a baseball game and the invitation was accepted. Countless times these reconnections lead to more work.

2. ANOTHER WAY TO RECONNECT. Look for articles on the company your friend or client works for and then call, or send an article and then call. Lead with this, "I've seen several articles on [your friend's company] recently and wondered how you're doing." It's that simple. Another variation on the same theme is to search the Internet for information on your friend or her company, then pick up the phone after finding something interesting. You're looking for a comfortable way to begin the phone call.

3. REGARDLESS OF THE PRETEXT OF YOUR CALL, MAKE A POINT OF ADDING VALUE DURING EVERY CALL. Does your client or friend learn something valuable every time he meets or talks with you? Before calling your friend, ask yourself "Whom can I introduce [your friend's name] to who might be able to help him?" Once you've thought of someone, pick up the phone with the purpose of exploring your friend's interest in meeting or talking to the person you have in mind.

4. CALL YOUR FRIEND OR CLIENT BEFORE THE NEXT INDUSTRY CONFERENCE YOU ARE BOTH LIKELY TO ATTEND. Suggest that you meet for breakfast or dinner while at the conference. Even if she tells you she is not going, it gives you the perfect excuse to reconnect by telephone.

5. IN LIEU OF A PHONE CALL, TOUR A CLIENT'S OPERATION OR VISIT AS OFTEN AS YOU CAN. There are a large number of rainmakers who swear this is their finest marketing tool. As many rainmakers have learned, "The more I see them in person, the more work I get." The general counsel of a telecom company related her experience as a young lawyer to me. When she was an associate, she always made a point of meet-

ing with clients on their turf rather than in her office. She was a trial lawyer focusing on workers' compensation cases. Rather than interview witnesses by phone, which was standard operating procedure for her peers, she'd conduct the interviews in person. This practice led one client to direct his insurance company to send all his company's future cases to this associate. This same client started calling her for employment-related questions too. By the time she left private practice to go in-house with a major telecom company, she had obtained a dozen clients that way.

6. MAKE CONTACT SOON. Perhaps it's the chase for more billable hours, but the sad truth is that most professionals don't contact their clients within two months after the deal or file is closed. It's the rainmakers who excel at staying in touch with their dormant clients. Often six months or more go by without any contact. The irony is that the longer it's been, the greater the discomfort in reconnecting. To prevent that, try this next time you finish your work: write down on your calendar: "Call [client's name] on October 29th." (that is, within a month or two after the closing). Some professionals say, "My clients know how to find me if they need me." This passive approach is *not* a formula for success. Don't wait for your clients to call you! Instead, take the initiative and call them! Clients appreciate these calls because it demonstrates you care about them beyond the scope of the current work.

7. CALL AND INVITE CLIENTS TO YOUR UPCOMING TALK. Many professionals find this is the perfect pretext for calling dormant clients and friends whom they haven't spoken with in some time. Not only can you invite them to your talk, but you can ask for their ideas on what they'd most like to hear on the topic.

When professionals are hesitant about calling someone they haven't spoken with in a long time, I have them make two calls. The first can be solely to re-establish the connection and allow for a warm-up. The second call can happen a month or two down the road and might involve a meeting or an invitation to attend your talk or whatever reason works for you.

One professional hadn't spoken to his contact for 18 months and had never had lunch with her. So, he felt it would be strange to suggest lunch during his first contact in 18 months. While he was unwilling to suggest a meeting on his first call, he did feel comfortable making contact several months later and suggesting a meeting.

Of course, the best way to stay in touch is never to lose touch in the first place. Too often that lesson is learned after you've lost touch with someone. In my view, the relationships we've formed over a lifetime are not trivial. Reconnecting with old friends and clients is deeply satisfying for most of us and helps us reconnect with parts of ourselves that keep us sane and grounded. Deciding to make the call and actually making the call are two very different things. Within the next 60 seconds, pick up the phone and call someone who hasn't heard from you recently. You're likely to make his or her day.

Set your intention to build friendships with fellow board members, and you're 90 percent of the way toward achieving them.

31

BUILDING RELATIONSHIPS WITH BOARD MEMBERS

HOW DO I DEVELOP BUSINESS RELATIONSHIPS WITH BOARD MEMBERS?

Many senior professionals are drowning in high-level contacts through their service on not-for-profit and other charitable boards. Yet most never parlay these high-level connections into business. Most board meetings leave little time for socializing before or after the meetings. As a result, many professionals end up having known fellow board members for years, but have little or no contact with them outside the board room. Many are flummoxed about how to leverage these high-level contacts because no one ever showed them how it's done. This chapter is your roadmap on how it's done. (It's so simple that even the most marketing-phobic professionals will be able to act on these ideas.)

The board meeting itself is an awful place to try to build a business relationship. Trying immediately before or after the meeting isn't much better because there isn't enough time.

Be sure that your board service is exemplary or you won't stand much chance of developing a professional relationship with other board members. Most professionals oscillate between two extremes: Either they do nothing to build a business relationship or they try to get business from their contacts prematurely. Most opt for doing nothing because they don't want to be accused of taking advantage or have people question their reasons for being on the board in the first place. There is a middle ground that most professionals don't consider: Single out one person at each board meeting and ask that person whether he or she will meet outside the confines of the board. This method can work in a variety of settings, including your golf or social clubs.

What follows is a proven and simple method for making the most of these kinds of high level contacts. Follow this method and you will establish more rewarding business relationships with fellow board members than ever before:

1. CHOOSE A PERSON. Decide in advance of your next board meeting who you want to invite to lunch, breakfast, or a cup of coffee. If you don't make the decision before you go, you may well chicken out. It doesn't allow you time to prepare. In addition, you are allowing fate to guide your marketing. I'm not big on letting fate be your primary marketing tool.

2. DO SOME RESEARCH. Do your homework on the company or the person targeted. This step is very important. Write out the question(s) you will be asking him or her in the next step.

3. APPROACH THE PERSON. In the minute or two of kibitzing that happens before or after your board meeting, make a point of seeking out this person and proposing the idea of a meeting. For example, you might say, "I've served on this board with you for five years and I know very little about your business. I feel bad about that. Would you be willing to meet for lunch some time in the next few weeks so I can learn more about your business?" This isn't meant to be a script. It's simply one way to do it. Most people, even very busy ones, will

be flattered by your request. There are a host of reasons why they may not accept your invitation. So if they decline, be sure to lay the foundation for asking again at another time.

The ideal ending to this 30-second or one-minute conversation isn't to get your calendars out on the spot and book a meeting. Instead, it usually involves that person's assent to letting you call his or her secretary the next day to arrange a meeting.

4. FOLLOW UP ON YOUR COMMITMENT. Call the very next day. These kinds of promises are cavalierly made and rarely kept. Do what you said you would do. Always. No exceptions. Ever. Write a note to yourself or put something in your calendar or PDA to call so you won't forget. Your credibility will suffer if you say you'll call the next day, but don't. Making promises and failing to keep them is bad marketing no matter what the circumstances.

5. PREPARE FOR THE MEETING. If you've gone this far, don't blow it by winging it at the meeting. It is very insulting to the person you are meeting. Write out on paper that person's personal needs and the questions you intend to ask.

6. HAVE THE MEETING. You are certainly encouraged to talk about board-related issues, but don't stay stuck on that for the entire lunch. For ideas on how to move beyond a casual discussion see Chapter 27, "Networking One-on-One."

The rainmaker at one firm followed this process with two board members he'd known for years and was amazed at how well it worked. He had meetings with both and parlayed one of those meetings into work. He feels the other board member is a likely prospect for work in the future. He found approaching them very easy to do once he knew how. Now that he has a stand-alone relationship, it will be much easier to meet again.

Do this with one person each month on a 12-member board and you will have a deeper relationship with the entire board in one year's time. If you have interest in doing this with just three of the 12 board members, you can achieve that objective in three to four months. What we're after is a stand-alone relationship with each board member outside the confines of the group. Like most other skills, this seems obvious after the fact.

During your next conference, act like a host, not a guest.

32

CONFERENCING WITH A PURPOSE

How Do I Get the Most Marketing Mileage out of Conferences?

Many professionals attend one or more conferences each year, but rarely do you hear anyone raving about them being marketing bonanzas. That's partly because they attend too many competitor-attended conferences and not enough client or industry conferences. Don't expect to generate much work from conferences of your peers unless you get most of your referrals from competitors. You'll get a much higher return on your time invested if you go to client and/or industry conferences. If you have never attended a conference with your best client, you'll be pleased to discover how great the bonding experience can be. It can also be an incredible chance to meet new people and learn more about the client's industry. While you're there, ask your client to introduce you to other people within the industry. Even if she is hesitant about introducing you to competitors, see if she feels comfortable introducing you to suppliers and others she knows who are not competitors.

Much like networking, this is another activity toward which great amounts of time and energy are expended, but that tends to deliver very little return on time and money invested. Many professionals view conferences as a free firm-paid vacation or a complete waste of time. It doesn't have to be either. The only ones who actually give much thought to conferences before they go are the rainmakers in a firm. From my work with thousands of professionals, I've found that you can get much more from each and every conference if you approach it with a game plan.

HAVE A GAME PLAN

What is your goal for attending the conference? The purpose of any conference is to start or deepen relationships with people who attend the conference. Pick a number that is realistic for you, whether it's to meet two or 20 people.

Professionals who set a tangible goal get more out of each and every conference than those who just wing it. One lawyer had spoken at a conference in the previous year. He wasn't scheduled to speak again during the next year's conference, but he wanted ideas on how to maximize his efforts. His coach suggested he recontact those people from last year whom he really connected with and ask whether they were going again this year. He loved that idea. He also liked the idea of asking a handful of his clients if they were planning to attend. At first, his goals for the conference were fuzzy. He eventually set an ambitious goal: Create relationships with at least 30 attendees at the conference. He may not achieve this goal, but even if he comes up short, he gains far more from that conference than the person who sets no goal.

While it may seem counterintuitive, never go to a conference with the goal of getting work. Why? You will come across as pushy or desperate. Remember, we want to start a relationship with people at the conference that will endure beyond the conference.

NO FIRM FUNDING WITHOUT A PLAN

Lack of a clear goal or purpose is one common reason why firms will refuse to pay for your attendance at conferences. One professional requested permission from the managing partner for funding to attend a conference in another city and was flatly turned down. Her coach suggested she ask again, only this time spell out who she intended to meet during the conference and how she would follow up after returning so she could show her managing partner the game plan. This chapter contains a wealth of ideas on how to justify to firm leaders that you are serious about the conference.

Now that we have a goal, let's outline how to achieve it. Think of a conference in much the same way as we approach other marketing activities: What to do before, during, and after the conference. Let's take them chronologically:

BEFORE THE CONFERENCE

1. GET A LIST OF ATTENDEES. An Atlanta lawyer obtained a copy of the attendees list for an upcoming conference and learned that one of her Atlanta-based clients also had another 10 people from that client's Charlotte office who were scheduled to attend. She made a point of meeting the Charlotte-based people while at the conference.

Some conferences will not provide you with the current year's list of attendees. In that case, last year's list will have to suffice. Examine the list several weeks in advance of the conference and formulate a plan of who you most want to meet. Make a dozen or more phone calls to the most desirable people on that list. During the call, set up as many breakfasts, lunches, and dinners as you can. For ideas on how to handle yourself during these meetings see Chapter 27, "Networking One-on-One."

If you can't find a list before the conference, pore over the list of attendees that's included in your registration materials once you get there and make a list of three or four people whom you'd like to meet. I keep this list in my shirt pocket so I can easily refer to it during the networking events that are part of the conference.

2. MAKE A HANDFUL OF PHONE CALLS. If your goal is to start a relationship with people in attendance, consider starting a dialogue before you get there by making a handful of phone calls. Even if you see the same people year after year,

call them. Ideally every breakfast, lunch, and dinner is booked during the conference. Here are categories of people you might want to call before your next conference:

- Clients (particularly those you've never met in person)
- Dormant clients (clients you've done no work for in the past several months or years)
- Referral sources (particularly those you've never met in person)
- Peers from different countries
- Prospective clients (particularly those who are based in another city)

The lawyer mentioned above contacted her Georgia contact and invited him to lunch so she could get the scoop on the Charlotte counterparts. It turns out he didn't know much about them, but he did give her the green light to say he "strongly suggested they meet."

3. CALL ONE OR SEVERAL OF THE CONFERENCE SPEAKERS. Call speakers who are presenting topics that sound interesting to you and ask them about their talk. Once you're there, seek them out again just before or after they speak. After all, speakers are potential clients too.

4. CALL OTHER PROFESSIONALS OR CLIENTS. Check for those who coincidentally live in the city where the conference is being held and arrange a meeting during your visit. Even if they aren't attendees, there is real value in hooking up while you're in their city. Building lasting relationships works much better in person than by phone or e-mail.

DURING THE CONFERENCE

1. SEEK OUT THE PEOPLE YOU CALLED IN ADVANCE. Track down clients (and others) whom you have never met in person while you're at the conference and make a point of meeting face-to-face. I have personally done this and found it invaluable for getting prospective clients over the hump of deciding whether or not they will hire you. It's also far more likely to result in a relationship that endures beyond the conference.

One of my clients had breakfast with someone who was a controller at his company. The controller was shy and reserved during breakfast, but it didn't stop him from making an introduction for her later in the conference.

2. MEET THE NEW CHAIRPERSON. If you're interested in speaking next year, make a point of meeting the conference chair for next year. See Chapter 33 for how to approach that conversation. In any conference there are always a small number of people who know everybody and serve as unofficial hosts. Do everything you can to find out who those people are and make a point of introducing yourself.

3. SPONSOR A DINNER. Host a dinner at THE restaurant where everyone loves to dine. Make the reservation several weeks before the conference. During all networking events at the conference, be on the alert for people you want to invite to join you for dinner. Befriend the orphans and forlorn looking ones. Once you know who is going to that dinner, prepare your list of questions in case you are seated next to any of them.

4. ENGAGE IN HIGH-ENERGY CONVERSATIONS. Rather than revisiting this at length, see the networking chapters in Part D.

5. SPONSOR A FOURSOME AT THE GOLF TOURNAMENT. If your firm is sponsoring several golf foursomes and one team needs a fourth, you can use that opportunity to ask each person you meet to fill in as the fourth. The prospective clients who love golf will be thrilled by the invitation.

6. PUT PEOPLE TOGETHER FOR THEIR MUTUAL BENEFIT. Rather than revisiting this at length, see the networking chapters in Part D.

7. USE THE COMPANY NEWSLETTER. If your firm publishes an electronic or paper newsletter, use it as a basis for getting people's business cards and e-mail addresses during the conference. Ask for permission to add them to the distribution list. If you happen to be writing or researching an article, this

gives you another way to approach the conference. Wearing your researcher's hat, ask each person you meet for input on the topic you are writing about. For more on this see Chapter 36, "Making Publications Pay Off."

AFTER THE CONFERENCE

1. ALWAYS IMPLEMENT *AT LEAST ONE* IDEA. What have you learned during the conference that pays for the trip? This idea might come from one of the seminars or an informal conversation with any variety of people.

2. MAKE A HANDFUL OF PHONE CALLS TO FOLLOW UP. If you had a high-energy conversation that was interrupted during the conference, you can pick up where you left off. Call a handful of people you met to whom you felt a strong connection. This works well with people you met who are based in another city.

Another client of mine, Gerald, who is based in Chicago, was not sure how to follow up after a recent conference in Washington, D.C. He had made great connections with several people. He hit it off particularly well with Carol, who was based in New York and had a more senior position. He was not sure how to continue a relationship with someone like Carol and feared that the connection would be lost if he did nothing. He decided to call Carol and ask her these three questions:

- "Are there other conferences you might suggest I attend?"

- "Do you have any plans to be in Chicago in the next few months?"

- "I'm wondering if you have any ideas on how to build my practice?"

3. OFFER SOMETHING OF VALUE DURING EVERY FOLLOW-UP CALL. For example, suppose you're from Seattle and the person you call is from Detroit. You could offer your firm's conference room as a base camp should she ever get to Seattle.

The measure of a successful conference isn't only how much you learned or how many business cards you collected; it's how many enduring relationships you cultivated while attending the conference. There is no guarantee that you'll meet the client of your dreams using these ideas, but I'm confident of this: You'll have a more productive conference and you'll meet more people than you did during last year's conference. You'll also achieve one other result: You'll have more fun.

PUBLIC SPEAKING, PRESENTATIONS, PUBLICATIONS

Don't spend much time educating your competition.
Look for opportunities to speak to audiences teeming with
prospective clients.

┌─────────┐
│ **33** │
└─────────┘

GETTING IN FRONT OF
THE RIGHT AUDIENCE

How Do I Find Choice Speaking Engagements?

Many professionals who enjoy public speaking want to know how to line up quality speaking engagements. In coaching countless professionals on doing just that, it is helpful to have them follow some simple guidelines. At worst, following these steps puts you in touch with your clients and allows you to have a conversation with them outside the realm of your current work. At best, you'll find yourself speaking to a room full of prospective clients.

FIND A TOPIC YOU FEEL PASSIONATELY ABOUT

Some introspection will, of course, help. If you're unwilling to look inward to determine which topics excite you, then you should scale back your expectations. Selling is the transfer of enthusiasm. If needed, research the topic to fill in any gaps in knowledge you have about the topic. Part of that research might include subscribing to publications that your target audience reads. I've found that the teacher isn't ready unless and until he or she feels a strong sense of passion about the topic.

LET YOUR CLIENTS GUIDE YOU TO THE RIGHT AUDIENCE

Decide on the right audience. (An exception to this applies to those professionals who are novice speakers. In that circumstance, speak to anyone who will listen so you can perfect your speaking skills.) Finding the right audience may seem difficult, but it need not be. What should you do? Go talk to several of your clients and ask them which conferences are the best ones in their industry. This gives you the added benefit of making another contact with your client beyond the immediate work you are handling. It also gives you a way to stay in touch with clients who are out of state. You ordinarily won't want to talk to a room full of your competitors, unless you have a unique practice area such as tax or bankruptcy. You'll want to speak to an audience where your ideal clients congregate.

LEARN WHICH ORGANIZATIONS YOUR CLIENTS BELONG TO

Inquire of two or three of your clients what groups they belong to. Ask their opinions of the groups. Most clients are flattered when you ask for their opinions.

FIND OUT WHEN AND WHERE THE NEXT CONFERENCE IS

Ask your client when and where the next annual or regional conference is set. If it's more than six months away, you might be in time for this year's conference but you should act fast! If the conference is less than six months away, you should probably be thinking about getting on the agenda for next year.

CHECK WHETHER YOUR CLIENT KNOWS THE CHAIRPERSON OF THE SPEAKERS' COMMITTEE

Ask if he or she knows the chairperson of the speakers' or conference committee or at least knows this person's name. If he or she knows the phone number, so much the better. If your client doesn't have the number, ask your librarian to look up the group in the Directory of Associations. This directory can be found in almost any local library.

SEEK CLIENT OPINIONS ON TOPICS YOU MIGHT WANT TO SPEAK ABOUT

Ask your client's opinion of a particular topic (or better yet see if he or she is interested in co-presenting). Ask if his or her fellow members would find topic X to be of interest. Be very specific about a topic. Some professionals worry that using this approach will limit their chance for success. Usually what happens is the reverse—the client suggests other topics that would be of interest.

See if your client is well-connected enough with the group to sponsor you as a speaker. If so, he or she can handle the next step.

SPEAK TO THE CHAIRPERSON OF THE CONFERENCE OR SPEAKERS' COMMITTEE

Once you've identified the name of the organization holding a conference, call the chairperson and ask her if she thinks the members would find topic X to be of interest. (Yes, it's the same question you asked your clients.) Making this phone call can be the most challenging part of this process. For that reason, I suggest you write out a short synopsis of your talk before you place the call so you are clear about what makes your topic relevant and interesting to the group. Ideally, the feedback previously gathered from your clients can be helpful at this stage. You might even run the summary by your clients.

If the chairperson expresses interest, be prepared to send her a one-to-two-paragraph synopsis of your talk that would be used to describe the program to members. The more generalized your approach to this call, the less effective you will be. Instead of saying, "Gee, I'd like to speak to your group," or asking "Are you looking for speakers?" ask her, "Do you think your members would find topic X to be of interest?" If you have audiotapes of previous speaking engagements or articles you've written on the proposed topic, make copies and send them to her. Be ready to provide speaking references. Some conferences require a proposal and application six to 12 months in advance. Do whatever it takes.

Follow Up After You've Sent the Proposal

As with most things in the marketing arena, follow-up is crucial. Be sure to end the conversation by learning the timetable on which the chairperson will decide on speakers for the upcoming program. Get her permission to let you call back in a set time frame if she doesn't call you sooner. Write that action into your calendar so you don't forget to make the follow-up call. Then do it.

The purpose for speaking is to start a relationship
with the people in the audience.

34

USING SPEAKING TO WIN NEW CLIENTS

HOW DO I GET CLIENTS FROM MY PUBLIC SPEAKING?

There are many effective tools in your marketing repertoire. One I see being used, and frequently misused, is speaking. I have met countless professionals who have given up on public speaking as a marketing tool after having spoken dozens of times. They claim it doesn't work. Don't believe it for one second. There are very few marketing activities that deliver a higher payoff if you know what you're doing. Keep in mind one very simple mantra if you're going to use speaking as a marketing tool: The purpose for speaking is to start a relationship with the people in the audience. Here is how to do that.

BEFORE YOU SPEAK

1. CHOOSE YOUR AUDIENCE WISELY. Is it teeming with your clients and prospective clients? If not, don't expect much business to flow from it. Too many professionals speak to an audience full of their competitors. This results in making your competitors more savvy about your topic and not much else. This won't deliver more work, unless most of your work comes through referrals from competitors. If you are an employment lawyer practicing with a large firm, don't speak to groups of

private practitioners. Try instead to speak to groups that contain large numbers of human resource professionals or senior executives. Seems obvious, right? Think back to the last time you spoke. Who was in that audience? I'll bet for many of you the audience was teeming with your competitors. The only other group of people who should be speaking to their competitors are your junior people, those who use speaking for credentialing purposes.

2. SPEAK ON A TOPIC YOU ARE PASSIONATE ABOUT. Not only is the audience important, but your message is too. That's why your message should feature your passion for the topic. Without that passion, you won't leave a lasting impression. If you've recently obtained a great result for a client, this might be the perfect topic for your talk. If not, select a topic you passionately believe in and that is timely.

3. SET A TANGIBLE "RELATIONSHIP" GOAL BEFORE YOU SPEAK. I always urge my clients to set some kind of tangible goal before they speak. In coaching one of my clients who is an environmental expert on an upcoming speaking engagement, I asked her what her goals were for the talk. Her goal was to "increase my visibility." I replied, "That's nice; what else?" She was stumped. I suggested she work to create five new relationships (preferably client relationships) from her speaking opportunity. Setting that kind of concrete target never occurred to her. Even if you don't achieve the goal, your behavior before, during, and after the talk will be more focused.

4. INVITE A DIALOGUE WITH THE AUDIENCE. Putting people to sleep is not a good marketing tool, so make sure your talk is vibrant and interactive. I'll bet that 99 percent of you use lecture as your primary method of getting your message across. Too many professionals are deluded into thinking that the purpose of speaking is to convey information. As a result, all their preparation time is spent on the technical aspects of the topic. While this is important, it completely misses the mark as to what they should be doing to prepare. Next time try something different: Engage your audience in a dialogue. How do you do that? Think of great questions you want to ask

the audience that will stimulate a group discussion. Not just any question will do. Ask only those questions for which most members of the audience are dying to hear answers.

One of my clients spoke to a group of doctors. His topic was "co-management." He started his talk by asking, "How many are using co-managed care?" Two-thirds of his audience raised their hands. Then he asked, "How many checked with your lawyer or the state to be sure it's legal in your state?" Only two hands went up. At the end of the session, he was mobbed with requests for information. One of the doctors who attended this session even went back to his office and told his lawyer (practicing in another state) to call the speaker. He eventually was hired by this other lawyer to give an opinion letter on the doctor's situation.

Questions are more likely to lead to a dialogue with the audience. And your ability to customize your remarks goes up exponentially by doing so.

5. MAKE YOUR PRESENTATION A CALL TO ACTION. I challenge the professionals I'm coaching to go well beyond conveying information. Instead, I want them to energize their audience to the point of taking action. Getting people to that level requires a solid mastery of the topic and provides a built-in bias toward action. Another one of my clients, a tax professional, spoke to a group of loan servicers. During her talk she described many fact-based scenarios that were similar to the situations she knew they were facing. This led to a barrage of questions from them and ultimately led to considerable new business.

6. OFFER A GIVEAWAY. Design a giveaway that you will offer at the conclusion of your talk. You want whatever you offer to cause you to be mobbed with requests for the freebie at the end of your talk. I offer to add people to my monthly electronic newsletter for free. This has several advantages. First, they will come up and talk with me in person. This allows for a one-to-one connection. Second, by their signing up for my newsletter, my name shows up on their desktop every month. Even if they hit the delete key, they are more

likely to remember my name or call me if they need a business relationship coach.

7. CALL YOUR TARGET AUDIENCE. Another frequently overlooked preparation step is calling a representative sample of your target audience (including both people whom you have never met and existing clients) to ask for their input on what areas they would like to see covered. This can be done months or weeks in advance of your talk. This not only gives you a legitimate reason to call on total strangers you've always wanted to meet, but it also allows you to create some buzz for your speaking engagement. Be sure to invite them to your session or offer to send them materials that will be handed out at the session if they can't come.

An Arizona OSHA lawyer was scheduled to speak at a general contractors meeting in Nevada. He wanted to expand his contacts in Nevada. He had spoken many times, but it had not occurred to him to contact people he didn't know and invite them to his talk. We discussed several actions he might take to expand his Nevada practice, including making calls to people in Nevada whom he'd like to meet and inviting them to his talk. He contacted four clients in Arizona who also had offices in Nevada and obtained the names of their Nevada counterparts. He called these contacts and invited them to attend his talk. During one of these calls, he learned the prospective client had just received an OSHA citation for $150,000. The prospective client came to the talk with the citation in hand and hired this lawyer after his talk. If he had balked at issuing the invitation, he'd never have had the work.

Call at least a handful (a dozen is even better) of clients, dormant clients, prospective clients, and people you'd like to meet and invite them to your presentation. Ask for their input on the topic. If this is done well, their feedback will actually improve audience receptivity to your message. Hundreds of professionals have found this step to be the perfect "excuse" to call dormant clients whom they haven't spoken to in years.

Most speaking you do will be unpaid. Ask conference organizers for three or four free conference passes as "payment" for speaking. Obviously, this won't work at a closed function where the person you want to invite isn't a member of the group. With these free conference passes in hand, call your clients and invite them to attend as your guests.

By doing this you can also start a relationship with members of the audience before you get there! Don't just send the brochure announcing your program. Three live phone calls are far better than 3,000 mailers. Remember, the goal is to start a relationship!

On the Day of Your Talk

1. ASSESS THE AUDIENCE. During the talk and immediately afterward you are assessing the audience. The people who raise their hands during the presentation and those who visit you immediately afterward at the podium are the best candidates for your follow-up efforts.

Your criteria for follow-up can be based on something as subjective as who you felt the strongest connection to or some other subjective factor. On a more objective level, you are trying to determine who are the most likely candidates for follow-up after your presentation. For help in sorting, consider where each client is in the buying cycle: Those who express dissatisfaction and a desire for a solution (explicit needs)[1] you should put first on your list for follow-up. Those who express dissatisfaction but don't state a desire for a solution (implied needs)[2] would come second on your list for follow-up. The wonderful thing about public speaking is that people will raise their hands and volunteer their problems. Those same people might clam up if they were to meet you in person on a sales call.

2. COLLECT BUSINESS CARDS FROM MEMBERS OF THE AUDIENCE. Make sure you collect business cards from those who fit the profile. Make a notation on the back of the card setting forth any hot button issue discussed. I met with one tax professional who had totally given up on public speaking as a marketing tool after having delivered dozens of presentations. With further probing I learned he was doing many things well. For example, he was always mobbed at the end of his pre-

sentations by people who asked him questions and wanted advice on the spot. After giving advice he would hand people his business card and invite them to call rather than asking for their business cards! He quickly realized this was a huge tactical mistake.

At the end of your presentation you will learn what value, if any, the audience places on your giveaway. If you're mobbed with requests for your giveaway, that's great. If not, think of offering something else when you do your next presentation. Keep experimenting until you get it right. Some professionals are stumped about what to offer and as a default offer their presentation slides to anyone who wants them. This is better than nothing, but it's lacking in creativity and originality. I prefer to offer my electronic newsletter for reasons stated previously.

3. GIVE ADVICE. Look for opportunities to give advice right there at the podium. This will come in two forms: Questions that can be answered in 30 seconds and questions that would take several minutes or more to answer. In the former situation, offer some advice and ask permission to follow up to determine how the advice turns out. In the latter case, explain that there is a line of people waiting to talk to you. In the alternative, explain your time constraints and your desire to know more. In either case, offer to call the next business day and discuss the problem in greater depth without charge. Too often professionals are stingy about giving advice until they are hired, but that is a tactical mistake. My belief has always been that if you can answer the question in 30 seconds you should do so.

4. MAKE A CALENDAR ENTRY FOR EACH PERSON. When you get back to your office, you must make a calendar entry (if you have a PDA you can do it right there at the venue where you speak) to call those people you've targeted for follow-up. If you don't, I'll bet you never follow up.

In an audience of 100 people, you might single out only one person from the audience for follow-up. Only in rare instances will you single out more than six or seven people.

We move on to the next and most critical marketing phase: follow-up.

After the Talk

1. Make all follow-up phone calls within 72 hours of your presentation. If you've done everything I've suggested to this point but fail to make follow-up phone calls, much of your effort will be for naught. Many of you are guilty of a very common but fatal assumption about speaking: Your work is done as soon as you leave the podium. In my view, you have done only one-third to one-half the work needed to transform members of the audience into satisfied clients.

Most professionals who speak do not think much about doing follow-up after their talk. Or they think about it but don't actually do anything. A helpful way to gauge your success is to make at least a handful of follow-up calls within three business days of your talk.

You must follow up with a phone call to those where it's justified. Your goal during each call is to set a meeting, because there is a much higher probability of forming a lasting relationship. One professional had a member of the audience come up to her with a follow-up question. She felt rushed in her answer. A few days later she started her call by saying, "I felt that we had to rush at the end and I wanted to be sure I answered your question completely." The client said, "It's a good thing you called; I have more questions and wanted to explore your coming and giving a similar presentation to my people."

How do you begin that follow-up call? Always lead with the need. The first words out of your mouth after identifying yourself (and where you spoke) should be a restatement of the need and an invitation to sit down with the former audience member in person to discuss her need. Out of the 100 people who sat in the audience, call first those people whose need is most pressing. And don't wait several weeks to call. If someone indicates she must take action within several days of your talk, waiting two weeks to follow up is far too long. If you were able to proffer advice, follow up to see if the person took it.

As stated earlier, most professionals think about calling, but never actually make these calls. They take the business cards collected during the presentation and put them on their desk (or worse, *in* their desk) and occasionally look at them with the intention of "some day" doing something with them. That day never comes, and eventually they throw them out.

2. MEET WITH THREE TO FIVE PEOPLE FROM THE AUDIENCE AND CONTINUE THE DIALOGUE STARTED ON THE DAY OF YOUR TALK. Prepare for the meeting as laid out in Chapter 17. Consider the shelf life of your name in the prospect's mind after your speech. If someone (who has never heard of you before) sees you speak, I predict it's measured in hours or days, not weeks, months, or years. The formula is pretty straightforward: Speaking does not equal a relationship. Speaking combined with a one-on-one meeting is more likely to create an enduring relationship.

3. OFFER AN ELECTRONIC NEWSLETTER TO MEMBERS OF THE AUDIENCE. If a meeting can't be arranged and they start receiving your electronic newsletter, you are much more likely to continue a relationship with people in the audience for the reasons previously mentioned.

If you start doing these things before, during, and after your speaking engagements, you will begin to see a dramatic return on your time invested in this activity. Try it. It works.

In high-stakes competitions, act like you are already the client's advisor.

35

THE SECRETS OF A WINNING PRESENTATION

How Do I Win More Beauty Contests?

These days, doing presentations, sometimes called "beauty contests" or "beauty parades," as part of a formal buying process is a fact of life. I field frequent queries on how to make winning presentations. More firms are figuring out and refining how to conduct these high-stakes competitions. There are even consultants who spend all their time helping professionals prepare for, and win, these competitions. What follows are several ideas you can use to ready yourself and your team for your next presentation.

What Can You Do Before The Presentation?

1. Notify the marketing department or marketing partner in your firm immediately! If your firm doesn't have such a person, ask a para-professional, staff person, or one of your partners for help. Your marketing director or other colleague can help you with the research. Not doing homework on the company is marketing malpractice. You will maximize your chances of winning by alerting your marketing director

or colleague to the RFP as soon as you know. The more time you allow to respond to the request, the better your chances of winning. It's a continuing source of amazement to me that so many professionals think about the marketing department or other less formal marketing assistance very late in the game, if at all. I guess some professionals assume that, as they are experts, their expertise extends to writing responses to RFPs. Of course, they're dead wrong. Professionals who think that way will lose.

2. START THE DIALOGUE BEFORE YOU GET THERE. Call your contact within the company that is hosting the competition. Develop a list of questions you'd like to ask of your contact beforehand. These questions should be directed to understanding the personal needs of the members of the panel. See if your contact will allow you to call other panel members to canvass their perspectives and needs.

When feasible, get permission to talk to everyone on the panel before the meeting. Prepare a list of questions for each panel member before you make each call so it doesn't come across as aimless. Here are two questions you might ask: "What is the business context for this project?" and "What kind of attention is senior management devoting to this matter?" All of this should be done with a view toward preparing your response and presentation to give them exactly what they're after. Calls to panel members will help you gain insight about what the criteria for selection will be. Under no circumstances should you do any selling!

Calling your contact ahead of time also serves another useful purpose. Sometimes these competitions are rigged, but how can you tell before you go? Easy. Request permission to speak to the people who are part of the panel. If they won't speak to you, I'd be very suspicious. If your contact speaks to you, but provides very little information about what the company needs, I'd be wary of it being rigged or tilted in someone else's favor.

3. DO A NEEDS ANALYSIS ON EACH MEMBER OF THE PANEL. If you know the CEO, CFO, CIO, general counsel, vice pres-

ident of human resources, and the president will all be in attendance, brainstorm a list of what each person needs. Don't be surprised if members of the panel have conflicting needs. Be very sensitive to those tensions.

4. PREPARE EVERYONE. Make sure each professional on the team knows his or her role during the presentation and be sure that each person has a list of questions to walk into the presentation with. The team that is best prepared asks the best questions. The team that asks the best questions usually wins the competition.

5. PRACTICE. Have the team rehearse and get feedback from the marketing staff or other professionals in the firm. Never skip this step if you want to win. The same advocates who always rehearse their presentations to third parties never think to prepare for a presentation to a client or prospective client. That's a huge mistake. Preparing for the presentation makes your team more spontaneous, not less. Be sure to rehearse as often as needed to get it right. Rehearsals will build the confidence levels of the less experienced members of your team. If necessary, rehearse the presentation again.

6. GET CREATIVE. Be prepared to offer creative fee arrangements that put some of the firm's "skin in the game." If the best you can come up with is your hourly rate, stay home. Very few high-stakes competitions will be won using the billable hour.

WHAT CAN YOU DO DURING THE PRESENTATION?

"What do I say or do once I'm there making the pitch?" I am asked this question frequently. As I've said before, telling isn't selling! If ever there is an occasion where professionals do too much telling and not enough asking, presentations are it. Go in thinking about starting a dialogue, not a monologue. You can't bore your prospects into hiring you. If your team speaks more than 50 percent of the time, it's probably hurting its chances.

One litigator was invited to a high-stakes contest where she met with a prospective client, including the CEO. She was skeptical of the strategy I had proposed, which was for her to ask questions. Her concern was that they were flying in from another city to meet her and hear what she and her team had to say and they had scheduled only 60 minutes to meet. In spite of her reluctance, she asked lots of questions and was amazed at how much the CEO wanted to talk. He ended up talking 90 percent of the time, and her team was hired! She found out that asking the right questions is very effective. It was a real lesson for her.

Verify the need first before pitching. Too many professionals go in pitching before verifying the need. Instead say, "It is our understanding that your primary concerns are A, B, and C. Is that correct?" In one case, the general counsel quietly listened to a pitch from a large firm that proposed to eliminate the general counsel's trial workload as first chair. The basic message was: "We will do everything for you. You won't have to spend your time litigating. You can do other more important things." Halfway through the presentation, the team learned the general counsel's bonus compensation was tied to the number of trials he conducted as first chair. Oops! Once the team learned this, they shifted gears and offered to make him first chair but still do all the work and allow him to gain much of the glory. This kind of error is totally avoidable if you go in asking rather than telling.

One law firm was invited to bid solely on trial work, but its presentation focused on getting intellectual property (IP) work. That's just plain dumb. The client didn't want to hear about the firm's IP capabilities; they wanted to hear about the firm's relevant litigation expertise. Needless to say, the firm irritated the daylights out of the panel and didn't get the work. Irritation is hardly a winning marketing strategy.

Give each person involved in the presentation a role and have him or her develop questions to ask of the panel. Make sure each member of the team has prepared two minutes' worth of relevant experience. I suggest each person have a set of questions to ask the panel if the opportunity presents itself. David Maister and his co-authors make a great point in their book *The Trusted Advisor*: If your time slot is one hour, go in prepared to give them the first hour of work on the engagement. I would add to that advice: Start acting as if you're already the panel's advisor. Don't force the panel to use their imagination on what it's like to have you representing them. Let them feel what it's like to have you on their team.

If junior people are involved, have them participate in relative proportion to how they'd do the actual work. If junior people will be doing 80 percent of the work, have them conduct 60 to 80 percent of the presentation. This is particularly important when the client insists that you bring the people who will actually be doing the work.

Start acting as if you have already been retained to provide services. By becoming well-informed about the prospective client's business, the nature of the project, and the needs of the decision makers, you are in a position to begin to deliver value to the prospective client.

One trial lawyer I worked with took these ideas to heart and sequestered himself in his office for two solid days to read through the voluminous pleadings of an ongoing lawsuit. The impression he made on the panel was very favorable and lead to almost seven figures worth of professional fees.

Last, get permission from the panel at the end of the presentation to follow up afterward. The panel may not always give you permission to follow up, but be sure to ask.

WHAT SHOULD YOU DO AFTER THE PRESENTATION?

Always follow up within a short period of time after the presentation. Write down when you will follow up into your calendar or PDA. If you don't write it down, I predict you will forget.

If you are selected, ask the client for the deciding factors that led to their hiring you. Too often, this step is skipped when we win. This feedback can help you win countless more contests.

If another firm is selected, ask for feedback on how you came up short. This is the ultimate tool for learning how to improve for the next presentation. Remember to ask questions, such as: "How did you decide to hire the firm you selected?" "Is there anything we could have done differently?" and "How did we come up short?" This step is crucial if you don't want to keep repeating the same mistakes in future presentations.

If you do your job right, you can avoid beauty contests. I have helped countless professionals stay out of high-stakes competitions altogether. If you can't avoid them, however, follow the steps discussed above and you will start winning more of these contests.

Use the article you've written to invite a dialogue
with clients and prospects.

36

MAKING PUBLICATIONS PAY OFF

HOW DO I MAKE PUBLICATIONS PAY OFF?

Professionals frequently want to know how they can make the articles they write or the articles they are quoted in "pay off." My answer is very simple: Use the article(s) as the basis for starting a conversation with people in your network or target market. You might even consider co-authoring an article with a client.

Most professionals write articles for credentialing purposes. We want to be known as authorities in our fields. This is particularly important for younger professionals, who are trying to carve a niche for themselves. Many professionals also write articles as a cornerstone of their marketing efforts. I'd advise against that. The time spent writing an article is rarely the best use of your limited marketing time. (One exception might be sending electronic updates that are chock full of insight to thousands of people in your target market at the push of a button.) Most professionals would be better served to spend two hours meeting with clients, dormant clients, prospective clients, or their partners. That's because building relationships is far more likely than authoring articles to land new work. Both the articles you write and ones in which you are quoted as an expert can be used as dynamite marketing tools if you think of them as catalysts for a dialogue.

BEFORE YOU WRITE AN ARTICLE

Use the article to invite a dialogue with people before it's written. You can call clients, dormant clients, friends, and prospects before you write it as part of your research. Your purpose is to build a relationship using the writing of the article as a catalyst.

For example, suppose you're in the middle of writing an article on the new privacy regulations. You are well-served to do some research, but not the kind you might think. Instead of heading to the library, make some telephone calls. Call your clients, dormant clients, friends, and prospects as a "researcher." One professional had a 92 percent success ratio in getting meetings with top decision makers within his target audience while writing an article for a major magazine, all under the guise of doing research. Some of the people you contact will offer great ideas that you can incorporate into your article. This will have the added benefit of producing an article that is much more "real world" and practical. If your article touches on actual needs and problems, you will find yourself knee-deep in a substantive discussion about the client's business in under five minutes.

A professional who was writing an article in the local business journal sent her article around to several people (some of whom she barely knew) and asked for their reactions. By so doing she reconnected with six people. As she discovered, the article proved to be a great catalyst for discussions with those six people. More importantly, she gained a sense of momentum that spilled over to her other marketing activities.

AFTER YOU'VE WRITTEN AN ARTICLE

After it's written or published, seek feedback or "critiques." Become a feedback hound. If you don't make at least a handful (a dozen is even better) of phone calls to clients, dormant clients, friends, and strangers to ask for their input, you've squandered an opportunity. Remember: To gain maximum benefit from the article, use it as a basis for inviting a dialogue.

If you can't bring yourself to ask for feedback, send a note enclosing a copy. Make sure what you send is brief and to the point. An employment lawyer had his labor law article published in a law review. The kinds of articles that are published in professional journals are too long and academic for most busy executives. I urged him to write a brief summary (no more than a single paragraph) of the article and attach the entire article. He had sent the full article (before it had been summarized) to three people on his own initiative. He wanted to know what more he could do. I asked him how many people might find the summary of interest. He realized far more than three people might find it interesting and relevant. He hadn't thought to send it to two very important groups of people in his network: dormant clients and his own partners! He loved the idea and sent it off to both groups. Even if a dormant client tosses it in the trash, you end up back on his or her radar screen.

Once you've sent it, call each recipient and ask these types of questions: "Did you receive it?" "Did you have a chance to read it?" "Was it helpful?" "Do you have any questions that it doesn't answer?"

When You're Quoted as an Expert in an Article

If you've recently received some good publicity and are wondering how to gain maximum mileage from it, ask yourself this question: Which existing clients and prospective clients should know about this? You can use the good press or the article you have written to "invite a dialogue" with the marketplace.

One professional received some very favorable press on his area of specialty. The article made it clear that more large companies should consider doing the kind of transaction this professional was known for doing. The article positioned him as an expert and a pioneer on doing these kinds of transactions. Getting good press is one thing; getting the phone to ring as a result of that press is something else entirely.

Here's how you can make the phone ring. Send an e-mail containing the best portions of the article to clients, dormant clients, partners, friends, and prospects. At the end of your message leave a question such as, "Any reactions to this article?" or "Would you like a copy of the entire article?" or a comment such as "I'd be interested in your thoughts." There is no magic to the language you use, but it is imperative that you invite a dialogue. Sending an e-mail message rather than a letter makes it much easier for a client or prospect to hit the "reply" button and start a dialogue. You radically increase the ease of response.

What Can You Do when the Phone Rings?

Most professionals don't know what to do when the phone rings. When a reader of your article calls you out of the blue, what should you do? See if you can parlay the call into a meeting with the person making the inquiry. An environmental expert in California named Betty received a call out of the blue from the executive assistant to the president of a refinery. Neither the assistant nor the president knew Betty. The secretary left her a voice mail asking for reprints of her article since the faxed copy he had wasn't very legible. Betty called him back right away. He was impressed with her quick response. She agreed to send him a legible copy of the article, but it never occurred to her to suggest a meeting or conference call to answer any questions the article didn't address.

Upon further reflection, Betty realized she could have asked questions such as, "What prompted the president's interest?" or "Is there a specific question the president has?" A meeting might have been arranged through the president's assistant. If Betty were dealing with an assistant who was empowered to set up a conference call, she could have achieved the goal of starting a dialogue.

No matter what kind of "ink" you get, your practice is all about relationships. Of course, you can write articles and hope the telephone rings, but it's even better if you initiate contact. Your article gives you a comfortable and legitimate basis for calling everyone in your phone list.

OTHER
RAINMAKING
SKILLS

Change your mindset from "my clients have legal or accounting or engineering problems," to "my clients have business problems or opportunities that require them to call me."

37

TURNING PROFESSIONALS INTO ENTREPRENEURS

HOW DO I LEARN TO THINK LIKE AN ENTREPRENEUR?

Most professionals are inadequately informed about how businesses operate. Business ignorance is increasingly unacceptable to clients. Clients hate having to educate professionals on the subtleties of their business because it slows them down and diminishes the practicality of the advice they receive. Professionals could radically increase their marketing effectiveness if they did nothing other than ramp up their knowledge of a client's industry. For example, do you know how the Internet is affecting (actually a better word is disrupting) their business plans? If not, you had better start asking your clients that question. And keep asking it frequently.

I would suggest you faithfully read business periodicals such as *Fortune, Business Week, Inc., Forbes,* or *Fast Company*. All are excellent at helping you learn more about how business works. Reading articles won't turn you into an entrepreneur, but there are three attitudes professionals can adopt to make them more entrepreneurial.

DELIVER ON ALL YOUR PROMISES

The size of the promise is irrelevant. Either deliver on it or don't make the promise. One client of mine promised to deliver a summary of closing requirements for real estate transactions in his state. While my coaching obligations with that client had ended, my curiosity had not, so I called him almost a year later (actually there were several calls every few months) and he still hadn't finished it! Nothing reduces a client's confidence in you faster than failure to deliver on a promise.

BECOME OBSESSED WITH SPEED

A *Business Week* article reported that Richard Anderson, vice president of Internet sales and operations at IBM, wakes up every night worried about speed. His constant concern is, "Are we moving fast enough?" How many professionals in your firm think that way? Unless everyone does, it's not enough.

One trial lawyer accustomed to representing auto manufacturers recently had lunch with a friend who worked for a high-tech company. This lawyer was advised by his coach to forget about getting work from his friend. Instead, his coach encouraged him to focus totally on learning more about this high-tech company through his friend. He was blown away by how different this meeting was from previous meetings he'd had with the same person. He left that meeting with a radically new view of the business. He couldn't believe how differently the two industries (autos and high tech) operate. He learned that his friend wanted speed above almost everything else. I've heard one source liken doing business in the high-tech arena to trying to change a flat tire while the car is still moving.

More businesses are starting to move at Internet speed. Several business periodicals have even used the phrase "Internet year." What is an Internet year? According to several sources, one Internet year equals 2.2 months. That means changes that formerly took a full year to unfold now occur in a little more than two months. If you're thinking "So what?" you're not thinking like an entrepreneur.

Here are some questions you can ask clients that might help show your sensitivity to this phenomenon: "How can we be easier to do business with?" "Do we move fast enough for your tastes?" "Of all the firms you work with, is our firm the easiest to do business with?" "What have other firms done that we can learn from?" One professional asked her client for feedback on how other firms do at responding to their needs. The answer was, "If they don't get back to us quickly, we have to invent an answer." They will only invent an answer so many times before they'll fire you.

BECOME OBSESSED WITH WASTE

The Internet phenomenon is so attractive because it will squeeze enormous amounts of waste out of business operations. I rode on an airplane with a senior executive at Oracle. Larry Ellison, Oracle's CEO, had told the troops they need to wring $1 billion in costs out of their operations over the next 18 months. The Internet makes that very doable. Large companies that thought they had already extracted the lowest possible prices from their suppliers are saving huge amounts of money using the Internet to do it. I have no doubt that professional service firms can benefit from some of these same tools. More importantly, professional service firms should start asking their clients how they intend to use the Internet to reduce their operating costs. Their answers will be informative and, I predict, surprising. One professional spoke to his client about using an extranet as part of his service offering. The client got very excited about it and commented on how it would fit well with his company's transformation into a paperless office.

Opportunities abound for the professional who thinks like an entrepreneur. If every professional in your firm adopts these three attitudes, you'll run circles around your competitors.

Knowledge is becoming a commodity;
insight, however, will never be.

[**38**]

DIFFERENTIATING YOURSELF

HOW DO I DIFFERENTIATE MYSELF FROM MY COMPETITORS?

Every prospective client you have ever met has, at the very least, wondered: "What makes you different from your competitors?" More and more clients aren't just quietly wondering to themselves. Instead, more clients are bluntly asking professionals this question during beauty contests and other meetings. Yet, when I ask this question of professionals for the first time many are stumped and speechless. How would you answer the question? Most first-time attempts are filled with platitudes such as "We have more experience than other firms" or "We offer one-stop shopping" or some other equally ineffective answer.

Every professional and firm should devote considerable time to answering this question, given its growing importance. Start considering it, even before you graduate from professional school, and never stop asking yourself as long as you remain in the profession. For most practitioners, the best place to start is by asking this question of existing clients and other professionals in the firm. These two sources are safe, and you won't believe the insights they provide.

Here are some of the answers I commonly hear when doing this exercise with a group of professionals:

- "Many in our firm are former regulators."
- "I ran my own business."
- "We care deeply about our clients."
- "Our practice group knows the industry very well."
- "I speak fluent Mandarin."
- "We have great relationships with regulators."
- "We can send documents to clients in four different word processing formats."
- "An intellectual property lawyer knows how to write code."
- "I always follow up on my advice."

You should also be prepared to back up any statements with as many examples (preferably striking ones) as you can recall during your career to highlight your statements. Those same examples should also be included in your personal biography. The key is to demonstrate, not just tell people what it is that sets you apart. Don't say you care about your clients; show them that you care by doing your homework before you meet with the client, and then ask penetrating and insightful questions during your meeting based on that homework. Look for a chance to give away some of your work product. The marketing director of a large Chicago firm always advises professionals to go into a meeting prepared to give away four hours of work product.

The good news is that you have more unique qualities than you think. The bad news is that you're not going to like what the Internet is doing to the uniqueness of your practice. To the extent they aren't already, many aspects of delivering professional services will become commodities within the next 10 years. That will send the price you charge clients steeply downward.

Nothing will give you a bigger advantage than using technology as a primary means of differentiating your firm. Here are two examples: A large Detroit firm invested heavily in creating a firm extranet that clients can access. Its system contains around 120 applications that can produce hundreds of documents that are normally generated by the firm's professionals. Instead of needing professionals to produce a first draft, the client does the data entry. Different? You bet. And this firm hasn't yet figured out how to sell it to the marketplace. Even more striking is the fact that the professional who was the primary contact for one of the first clients to begin using this system left the firm, but the client didn't. The client's loyalty was tied more to the system than to the individual.

Don't think an Internet strategy only applies to large firms. There is a two-person accounting firm that produces financial reports for its clients. What makes this firm different is that it turns around finished product in less than 24 hours and does it at a cost of only 10 percent of what a typical firm charges. How? The firm has an army of 50 professionals in India who do the work while the two accountants are sleeping. This gives new meaning to the notion of making money while you sleep.

Suppose someone comes to your best client tomorrow and says, "What differentiates our firm is that we want our client to have as much control as possible over the production of the finished product. That means you get to enter the data from your desktop. Oh, and by the way, we can turn around the finished product in one day when the standard in the industry is two weeks. Oh, and I forgot to mention that it will cost only one-tenth of what most other firms charge." I bet you're thinking, "This won't happen in my area of practice." Even if that day hasn't arrived, it will likely be here much sooner than most of you think. I hope you are ready for that day.

*Indulge in activities with clients in which you possess
a shared passion.*

┌─────┐
│ 39 │
└─────┘

RANDOM ACTS OF GOLF AND OTHER RECREATIONAL ACTIVITIES

IS GOLF OR ANOTHER RECREATIONAL ACTIVITY A POOR USE OF MY SCARCE MARKETING TIME?

I'd predict that professionals squander more valuable marketing time on the golf course than in any other single activity. Some professionals use golf with prospects as the excuse to work on their game. I'm not against taking time off for recreation. That is both valuable and necessary. What I object to is deluding yourself into believing that just because you are on the golf course with a prospective client you are marketing. If you or a partner in your firm keeps taking the same prospective client out for a round of golf and never returns with business, that's not a good sign.

SHARED PASSION FOR THE GAME OR ACTIVITY

Many of the methods described in this chapter can be used for all sorts of other activities, such as fly fishing, the performing arts, mountain biking, and hunting, to name just a few. The key is finding prospective clients who share your passion for the activity. One rainmaker confided that a huge number of the clients he brought to the firm during his 30-year career were built around their shared passion for fly fishing.

Playing a round of golf (or these other activities) with a client or prospective client can be an extraordinary bonding opportunity. Unlike a lunch (which might take one or two hours), a round of golf involves a minimum of four to five hours. While rainmakers make effective use of this huge block of time, most professionals do little if anything with the opportunity. In fact, I'd say they undertake nothing more than random acts of golf.

If you want to avoid random acts of golf, there are several things you can do before playing your next round with a prospective client:

Write Out Some Questions to Ask

While you're checking to make sure you have enough golf balls to make it through the round, be sure to stock up on good questions you will ask of your playing partner. These questions can take the form of high-energy questions or simply questions designed to learn more about your golf mate's business. I won't rehash what those questions might be, since we've discussed them in previous chapters.

Have a mental outline of what topics you might like to discuss during the round. As with everything in marketing, you must listen carefully to another's mood. If your golf partner does not want to talk business, you have to respect that boundary.

Do Some Homework

Be sure to do some homework and due diligence on the person you are playing with or his or her company. I can't predict when the research will pay huge dividends, but I can predict that it will pay huge dividends, eventually. I have clients who parlayed a chance meeting with someone they met through a friend during a round of golf into a stand-alone relationship—all because they did a little homework ahead of time.

Use Common Sense on When to Discuss Business

Don't jump into a business discussion too quickly. I'd suggest you not raise any business discussions until you have a few holes under your belt. If the prospective client raises it sooner, so be it. Use your discretion when raising sensitive or painful business issues during the round. You might find it's better to avoid those issues altogether. For example, raising a painful business issue immediately following a poorly played hole may not go over so well and, in some cases, can retard the relationship-building process.

Getting Paired with Strangers

There is a vast difference between playing a round with a prospective client you invite and being paired with strangers at a public or resort course. You can plan out what you'll ask in the former situation. In the latter situation, you never know what reactions you'll get to inquiries about someone's work.

My sister, who works in broadcast television, detests it when people she meets on a golf course ask her about what she does. I happen to like that question. She and I represent two extremes. Remember, the range of sensitivities of the people you are paired with is equally vast. Some are very private and want to focus only on golf. Others are quite willing to talk business. One question I've found effective at getting people to open up is, "What do you do when you are not golfing?" This gives people an option to respond with a work-related answer if they want to. If they don't, you might hear an answer like, "I coach my ten-year-old son's soccer team" or some other non-business answer.

Making Great Use of Your Private Club Membership

Your membership in exclusive private clubs can be a huge magnet for meeting "unreachable" prospective clients. For example, if you know that a prospective client is an avid golfer and would love to play your private course, this is a wonderful relationship-building opportunity.

On the other hand, many of my clients lament seeing the top decision makers every week at their private club, but never moving beyond that stage. In these situations, the goal is to meet with fellow members in venues away from the golf course. It still involves doing homework, preparing questions, and usually a phone call to suggest a lunch or meeting.

One of my clients tried this with the CEO of an internationally known, privately held company in her region who belonged to the same country club. She loved this approach because it gave her a mental outline on how to do it comfortably. She had known the CEO for years, but had never figured out a way to move beyond the country club relationship. A simple phone call and a clear game plan did the trick.

Your passion for the game can generate referrals. Bill Cates is the author of a wonderful newsletter on referrals written primarily for financial advisors. His ideas are equally applicable, however, to other professional service providers. In a recent issue, Cates said this about golf and marketing:

> "I'd like to share [a] way producers have turned their love for golf into opportunities to generate new business and referrals. Jerry Grant not only loves golf, but has many clients who enjoy the game as well. Several times a year, Jerry hires a local pro (with a great reputation) to run private clinics for him and his clients. He invites a few select clients to attend, and he encourages them to invite one 'successful friend.' The clients understand what Jerry is trying to accomplish (meeting good prospects) and they enjoy the great golf lesson for themselves and their friends.

> "Everyone shows up for a lesson—which everyone enjoys. Then they hang out for a while for some golf talk and simple refreshments. Two things happen from these clinics. First, Jerry's relationships with his golf-playing clients are enhanced. Second, almost every clinic results in one or more appointments with new prospects."[1]

That sounds like an inexpensive and fun way to meet people and make new connections with clients and friends by capitalizing on your shared passion for the game.

Playing Golf Reveals Your Character

You can learn a great deal about a person's character by playing a single round of golf with him or her. Does he cheat and throw clubs? Or does she keep her cool when the bad breaks come? Not only can you gauge others, but they can assess your character as well.

I hope you've learned how to make this wonderful game an ally in your marketing effort. As many of my clients have discovered, it's possible to have fun, build incredible relationships, and accomplish your marketing goals on the golf course.

Marketing, at its highest level, is an act of service
to another human being.

┌─────┐
│ 40 │
└─────┘

MARKETING BY PROJECT-BASED PROFESSIONALS

CAN PROJECT-BASED PROFESSIONALS REALLY MARKET?

Most members of firm management throw their hands up in disgust when they contemplate teaching their project-based professionals how to market. These are professionals who sometimes say, "I don't have clients, I have projects" or "I don't have clients, I have cases." Almost without fail, such persons claim that marketing is tougher for them than it is for their colleagues who provide consistent or ongoing services for clients. While I agree it is different, I'm not willing to concede that it's tougher. I'll go one step further and suggest it can be lots of fun!

I believe most project- or case-based advisors are well-suited to becoming great rainmakers because they are already skilled in the arts of investigation and persuasion, particularly asking great questions, that is, doing their homework on the prospective client. Most don't realize these skills are critical to their success in marketing. If such professionals have one shortcoming, it's generally their poor listening skills. Those who become great listeners become great marketers. Those who don't will struggle.

Develop and use these skills of investigation, questioning, and listening in connection with the following seven things and your project-based professionals will improve their marketing.

YOUR BEST SOURCE OF WORK IS YOUR OWN PARTNERS

Be very focused when marketing internally. One trial lawyer from Canada took this idea to heart and met with several of his partners. These meetings generated five new lawsuits from his partners in a few months. In another case, a consultant in Texas was given a forum to speak to a group of her partners. Most professionals spend little or no time clarifying what they will say to their own partners. This lack of focus results in lots of rambling about what they do. This consultant had just been through an exercise in one of my workshops in which she was asked to describe her ideal client to one of her partners. She struggled with the answer to the question during my workshop, but was ready with a very precise answer during her presentation.

Instead of talking about what she does, she explained to her partners how she can help their public company clients! This was a radical departure from the usual presentations given by others. Results came immediately from this talk. One of her partners called 15 minutes after the presentation asking permission to arrange a meeting with a client who had an immediate need. Because this consultant had detailed her skills and favorite projects, her partner was better informed and immediately prompted to take action. There are so many opportunities like this within most firms it's mind-boggling.

THINK OF YOURSELF AS A BUSINESSPERSON FIRST
AND A PROFESSIONAL SECOND

Thinking as a businessperson, become a valued advisor to the people in your network. I urge all professionals to think of themselves as businesspeople first and professionals second. That single shift of mind will radically alter your effectiveness. After hearing this suggestion, one professional began thinking of his friends in business as professionals with a project backlog. His conversations shifted from purely social discussions to uncovering which matters caused them the greatest headaches. By shifting his focus in that way, he was able to offer ideas on how to alleviate the headaches. This also ties into another theme I emphasize constantly: Start acting like you are already their professional! Does your client or prospect learn something valuable every time she meets or talks with you?

What humbles many professionals is how little they know about their friends' business concerns. It's not too surprising when you consider how they spend their time during meetings. Here is a litmus test for the next meeting you have with a friend whom you think sees you as a business advisor: If you spend most of your time on social conversation (that is, the spouse, the kids, the dog, the latest exploits on the golf course), you're probably not an advisor. Many professionals wait until the check for lunch arrives before discussing business. That is a huge wasted opportunity. Much earlier in your lunch you should ask questions such as:

- "What are your goals for the coming year that the firm should know about?"

- "Anything we can do to help you achieve them?"

- "How has the Internet affected your business?"

- "What does your ideal customer look like?"

- "What trends worry you the most about your business?"

- "Who are your major suppliers? What are their needs?"

- "Which competitors do you fear most? Why?"

I often ask how many businesspeople he or she knows personally who are not clients. Generally, the answer I hear is two or three. If so, set a goal of doubling that number to four or five in the next six months or a year. If your primary hiring contact in companies is a senior manager, the question is, "How many senior executives do you know personally who are not your clients?" I hear similar answers: not many. When professionals ask me where they meet these kinds of people, I suggest they go to the small universe of people they already know and ask them where they congregate.

Become a Member of an Electronic Discussion List
These lists are popping up all over the Internet. If you don't know which list to join, ask clients if they belong to one, get the website address, and sign up. These lists have your target audience talking to each other about their day-to-day worries and concerns. In the digital age, it's nearly marketing malpractice to be totally cut off from these lists.

Look for Opportunities in Unlikely Places
Too many professionals think they don't have time for marketing when, for example, they spend all week doing a project in another city. That is rarely the case. It's more a matter of how you use the little time you have available. One professional recently proclaimed she didn't have enough time for doing more marketing. Further questioning revealed she had a full week of out-of-town meetings where her client would be in attendance. This was the perfect venue for trying out questions such as "What is the business context in which this project arises?" and "How do you expect the Internet to affect your business?" Such questions are excellent conversation catalysts during a dinner conversation. The real shift of mind is remembering to ask them. One lawyer was interested in targeting the adverse party involved in a lawsuit once the matter was concluded. She soon realized that some of her marketing due diligence could be found in answers given by senior executives during depositions!

Explore Their Other Business Concerns
Focus on learning what other needs your client has for the full range of services your firm offers. During one exercise I do in my Courting New Clients workshop, I ask professionals to think of as many possible outcomes ("advances") to a marketing meeting as they can muster. Many don't consider outcomes that benefit their partners! I would estimate no better than 10 to 20 percent of the professionals in any firm think of options that will benefit someone else inside the firm.

One professional service advisor met with a friend who

expressed an interest in raising capital. During our debriefing phone call, this professional realized he could have offered to introduce his friend to one of his partners with many contacts in the venture capital world. My client admitted that he sees himself too narrowly. He sees himself as a specialist only, and thus sometimes misses opportunities to converse in areas other than his specialty. The problem plays out in reverse, too; this is why you must market with great focus within your own firm.

Devise Topics for Your Speeches That Your Target Audience Craves. Then Invite Them to Your Talk

If you are slated to speak somewhere on a hot topic, start calling people within your own network and invite them to your talk. Or ask your partners for permission to call their clients and invite them to your talk. Go one step further and find out what they'd most like to hear about the topic. This often gets you into substantive discussions. One professional from the Midwest called 15 in-house professionals (some of whom were clients, although many were not) before he spoke to a national association convention. He wins big even if none of them show up for his talk because he started a dialogue with his target audience before he got there!

Become a Follow-Up Fanatic

Start giving out lots of advice and follow up on every piece of advice you give. This gives your phone calls more purpose. When you send articles or written materials out to people after a meeting or speech, immediately make an entry on your calendar a week or two down the road to follow up with a phone call. Ask four questions during your follow-up call: "Did you receive it?" "Did you have a chance to glance at it?" "Did it answer your question?" and "Would you like to meet to discuss it further?"

This is not an exhaustive list. If you're already doing several on a systematic basis, you're probably getting some results. If not, take the time to apply one or more of these ideas, and you will vastly improve your marketing.

LEVERAGING YOURSELF: WORKING WITH AND THROUGH OTHERS

Treat every person in the firm as if he or she were an unpaid volunteer, because in the final analysis that's what each one is.

41

FINDING AND KEEPING GREAT ASSOCIATES

How Do I Keep Great Associates?

Firms around the world constantly struggle to find and keep great associates. The shortage is particularly acute in hot practice areas such as mergers and acquisitions, trademark, copyright, and patent prosecution. Most professionals have a mechanistic view of people as being interchangeable, when they should view people more organically. Most professionals view their firms as great big, old-fashioned clocks that need the right number of moving parts to operate smoothly. If a spring or a cog breaks, no problem. Just replace it with another interchangeable part. Professionals forget that they are in the relationship business first and foremost. An organic view of people is far more accurate and likely to make you want to keep good people. In fact, you're more likely to want to develop good people into great ones. The organic view says professional service firms are more akin to the human body. It's an integrated system. You don't just hack off an arm and graft a new one onto the body without causing serious trauma. What can you as an individual do about this problem?

Much more than you might think. Here are four things that you can do to combat this problem:

TREAT RECRUITMENT AS A YEAR-ROUND ENDEAVOR

Too many firms tend to think in terms of a recruiting season. Perish the thought. The shortage of valuable associates is so acute that in my view it requires a year-round focus. Anything less than a full-scale year-round effort is likely to leave you coming up short on the talented people you need to delight your clients. The practice of year-round recruiting has been a staple in private industry since the 1990s, particularly those companies that recruit information technology people.

Your recruitment effort will improve dramatically if everyone in the firm knows what the ideal associate's characteristics are and stays alert to finding those people. The test for you is: "Do you know what the criteria for hiring associates are?" Don't be lulled into thinking that it's the recruiting committee's job to be on the lookout for great associates. It's everyone's job to be on the lookout for great associates and partners! Some New York City firms have resorted to paying their current employees $10,000 for each new associate who is hired through their initial introductions.

As tough as it is to find great people, it's even more difficult to keep them. My work requires me to gain insights about what motivates professionals. If you have an associate working for you now whom you really want to keep, take this quiz. Write down on a piece of paper the three things this professional values most about his or her work. Then go ask the associate; you may be surprised. Most partners struggle to answer this question. Or they guess. If you can't answer the question with a high degree of accuracy, you risk losing that person.

EXPRESS THANKS TO ASSOCIATES DAILY

The two secret weapons in the race to keep great associates are *appreciation* and *gratitude*. I sometimes hear senior professionals rave about how wonderful their associates are. I usually ask them if they have ever told their associates what they just said to me. The typical reply is: "Not in those words." I encourage them to tell their associates what they just told me. Professional service firms can at times be incredibly pressure-packed places to work. Words of appreciation and gratitude fall likes drops of soothing rain on dry and dusty soil. There is no more valuable gift than to say that you believe in someone.

Tell a professional who works for you or whom you are coaching that you think he has great potential. Even better, if you think he is capable of generating a specific amount of business, say so: "George, I am certain that you can generate $500,000 per year in business if you continue to faithfully apply this system." I've done this with numerous clients. They always amaze themselves when the fees come in at the revenue levels they set at my urging. Giving people a strong vote of confidence may be all they need to reach the next level in their marketing. If you only THINK it, but don't SAY it, they will never hear those transformational words.

Let me put it bluntly: Most associates and partners in professional service firms are starving for meaningful feedback. The irony is that most partners are not the least bit inclined to spend the time needed to give their associates valuable feedback. Many partners hide behind the fact that the firm doesn't pay them to develop people. That's simply ignoring reality. (In fact, some firms base part of their partners' compensation on associate productivity.) If you give feedback, there is an effective way and an ineffective way to do it.

You will become a better mentor overnight if you will simply follow this guideline: Any time you have a thought of appreciation or gratitude toward one of your associates, act on it immediately! That means if it's 9 p.m. and you just read the Motion for Summary Judgment prepared by your associate, pick up the phone and leave him a voice mail or send him an e-mail thanking him for his efforts. The sooner you leave the message after having the thought, the more lasting the impact. If you wait as little as one hour to act on your thought, you might not act at all, or the sincerity with which you express the gesture may be greatly diminished. The more specific you can be about what impressed you, the more powerful the reinforcement. Best-selling author Ken Blanchard is a big proponent of "catching someone doing something right and recognizing them for it."

Do the exact opposite with negative comments. Wait until you cool off; then ask your associate to assess his or her own performance. If he or she doesn't notice the deficiency, ask a question that guides him or her to it.

DELEGATE WORK TO THE ONE WHO WOULD MOST BENEFIT

What most professionals call delegation is actually abdication. Take this quiz: You have just been handed a new assignment by your client. It's a straightforward project that you've done dozens of times and can do in your sleep. You have three choices: You can choose to do the work yourself, you can get a first-year associate to do it, or you can hand it to a fourth-year associate who is swamped with work. Who gets the work and why? Some professionals are perfectionists and will do the work themselves. That's the worst of all choices. Many professionals will give it to the fourth-year apprentice because it won't take as long to delegate. No wonder associates jump ship! It's the rarest of professionals who will take the time to show the less-experienced professional how to complete the project, yet it's the most valuable to the associate, the firm, and ultimately to all the firm's clients served by that associate.

Developing great people is no accident. Most firms want to hire the proverbial genius who gets up-to-speed very fast and turns into a great professional almost entirely under his or her own power. Firms dearly want to recruit those people, but the sad fact is that they are always in seriously short supply. And even if you hire them, they may move on to another firm after two to three years of getting top-flight experience at a larger firm. While it may be possible to find associates who can develop their technical skills or people skills rapidly, it is the rare associate who develops both skill sets rapidly and with minimal coaching.

I recently had lunch with a young partner who had resolved to come into the office one hour earlier than had been his usual practice to undertake important activities that he normally couldn't get to during the course of the day. He also expressed an interest in developing one of his younger associates. I asked him how he was using that additional hour each day to develop this associate. He wasn't. It hadn't occurred to him to use a portion of that extra hour to map out a development plan and meet with this associate and consciously help her develop one new skill. What he realized was he had fallen into the trap of doing more of the same, only he started an hour earlier each day. Once this associate learns one new skill, she and this partner can work on a second skill until she becomes proficient and then move on to a third skill. Keep doing this and in a very short time you will have an outstanding performer.

Professionals who are effectively mentored are more loyal and jump ship less frequently. I've heard many partners argue that it doesn't make sense to spend time mentoring young professionals because many of them will leave the firm. That's a poor excuse. Most professionals who are developed properly are intensely loyal to their firms. An "Emerging Workforce" study reported in the March 1, 1999, issue of *Business Week* found that 35 percent of employees who don't receive regular mentoring plan to look for another job within 12 months. However, just 16 percent of those with good mentors expect to jump ship. With the right mentor, their ambitions can be fulfilled within your firm. Properly developed associates are far more valuable to you and your clients. Too many firms think only about how the loss of an associate affects them personally. What they forget is that when a prized associate leaves, the client loses too.

Associates who jump ship might also go in-house. I can't think of a better business development tool than to have a grateful associate leave your firm and go in-house. A well-treated associate who goes in-house will naturally do everything possible to send work to you. I see it happen frequently. The more astute professionals view the development of associates as the cultivating of their future client base. I've also seen the reverse: An associate goes in-house and makes a point of never hiring anyone at the old firm because he or she was treated poorly. Of this you can be sure: Associates who won't hire anyone at their old firm probably weren't provided much mentoring while they were at their old firm. Or it was mentoring of the unwanted variety, that is, all criticism and no reinforcement of things done well. Ineffective mentors should be called "the morale suppression team."

TREAT EVERY ASSOCIATE AS AN UNPAID VOLUNTEER

Treating associates as volunteers makes it far more likely that they will receive psychic benefits that people seek from their work, and thus will stay on the job. Sound preposterous? It's not. In order for someone to put forth his or her very best, it can't be coerced. How much must you pay someone to care deeply about the firm's clients? In the final analysis, everyone is a volunteer. Can you demand that people give the best of their talents by threatening them or paying them more money? In my experience, the answer is definitely not. People work for many reasons, among them psychic rewards. Treating associates as volunteers makes it far more likely that they will receive psychic benefits that people seek from their work. As one managing partner confessed: "We don't give enough attaboys to our people."

Some partners point out that they weren't treated that way as they were making their way through the ranks, so why should they treat their associates that way? Because it's the right thing to do. There is another reason too: Losing great people is very costly. I won't rehash all the studies that have done economic calculations of the hard costs of turnover. The soft costs are even greater. Clients hate the revolving door of associates they are forced to deal with at most firms. Losing good people devastates client satisfaction levels. Think about it: Many of your clients resent having to spend their valuable time and money helping your associates understand their business. If an associate leaves the firm just when the associate gets familiar with your client's business, this weakens the overall client relationship. If it happens frequently, it may well end the client relationship.

Recruit constantly; find things to praise in others; delegate work and teach; treat every young professional as if he or she were a volunteer. Start doing these four things today. If you do, your clients will win, your firm will win, your associates will win, and you will win, because the feeling of satisfaction derived from developing someone is priceless.

*Make a point of saying three thank you's every day
to members of your team.*

┌─────┐
│ 42 │
└─────┘

DEVELOPING ASSOCIATES

HOW DO I DEVELOP ASSOCIATES' MARKETING SKILLS?

Until firms start making the development of associates a top priority, most will fail miserably at developing the next generation of professionals. Given the starting salaries being paid at some professional service firms, some real investment in developing their talents would seem to be in order. Even if the firm never starts a formal program, there is something you can do. Adopt one associate today and make it your job to help cultivate his or her skills. Before you adopt one person for coaching, be sure he or she wants to be mentored. It must be a two-way relationship. The senior partner of one large firm asked an associate if he wanted to be a partner in the firm. There was a long pause before the associate replied, "I don't know." The partner said, "Come see me when you know the answer."

Regardless of what skills you are working to develop, make a point of saying three thanks you's per day. Most people are hungering for feedback and appreciation. The problem with most professionals is that they don't start giving feedback until their associates (and partners) have slid into extreme under-performance.[1] And when associates do receive any feedback, it tends to be negative. If the only time you open your mouth is to deliver negative feedback, then open your mouth less often. Make a point of telling people how strongly you believe in their potential and future with the firm. We all thrive on encouragement.

Here's a 30-day plan for developing the marketing talents of associates:

1. HAVE YOUR ASSOCIATES ATTEND SEVERAL MARKETING MEETINGS WITH YOU. Set up at least two marketing meetings and clear those meeting times with your junior professional so he or she can attend as well. Don't drag people along who don't want to go. It's been my experience that most associates are delighted to be asked. Those who beg off regularly because they're worried about their billable hours are telling you something about their long-term thinking.

2. SPEND TIME PREPARING. Before heading off to the meeting, prepare with the associate. It doesn't have to be hours. It might be only 15 to 30 minutes. The key is you must model preparation. It's critical to involve the associate in the preparation. Remember to prepare for your next marketing meeting with the same thoughtfulness you'd use to prepare for a hearing or negotiation. If the associate isn't involved, he or she won't have as much commitment to what's happening. No involvement, no commitment.[2] Tell the associate your objective for the meeting so you can both assess how you did.

3. GIVE YOUR ASSOCIATE A ROLE TO PLAY. This can be as simple as asking one question that shows he or she knows something about the prospect's business. One trial lawyer in Texas was invited to a high-stakes beauty contest where the client asked him to bring along the team he'd expect to have working on the case. During the preparation phase, I suggested to this senior litigator that he have the other two lawyers participate in the presentation in the same proportion as they would when actually handling the case. The younger lawyers played a significant role in the beauty contest, asking some pointed questions, and their team performance led to

the firm winning a role in the lawsuit. If the situation permits, ask your associate to take detailed notes. Also ask him or her to be vigilant about what the client is telling you about its needs. Where feasible, all professionals should head off to marketing meetings in pairs because there are two pairs of eyes and ears rather than just one.

4. DEBRIEF AFTERWARD. After the meeting, discuss what just happened. Let the associate talk first.[3] Start the debriefing by asking, "How do you think it went?" This is critical to learning. I can't tell you how many times lessons are learned after the fact. If you're a practice group leader, share those lessons learned again during your practice group meetings. If your rainmakers insist on telling stories, the best stories to tell aren't about their successes, but rather about their failures. When junior professionals in the firm realize that the firm's best rainmakers have made some real mistakes, the task of learning new skills seems more achievable.

Those who refuse to invest in their associates because they might leave the firm are engaged in very shortsighted thinking. First, people are less likely to leave an organization if they are effectively mentored. Second, even if they do leave, they will either go in-house, into another business, or to another firm. The first two scenarios might well generate new business for your firm. The latter scenario may still lead to work based on conflicts. Yes, you could end up competing against a former associate for the same work, but if you're good, what are you so worried about?

*In your role as coach, never end a conversation with
a professional without a time-dated commitment
to take specific action.*

43

JUMP STARTING OTHERS'
MARKETING EFFORTS

HOW DO I MOTIVATE OTHERS TO MARKET?

A firm whose leader can get everyone in the firm moving in the direction of firm goals is going to vastly outperform other firms. Motivating people to take action is one of those critical skills not taught in school. Nearly every firm I've worked with during the past few years has expressed a strong desire to get more of its professionals into the practice development game. Yet when I observe firm leaders or marketing directors conversing with associates or other partners, I notice there is a decided lack of effectiveness to these conversations. I rarely see these leaders getting commitments for action. Most people don't automatically move themselves into action. The typical firm manager has at least a handful of chances every day to propel people into action. Don't waste those opportunities. If you're serious about results, have more conversations for action. Never lose your focus on getting professionals to take action. There are six steps needed to hold a conversation for action:

1. **ASK THE PERSON TO DESCRIBE AN ACTION HE OR SHE IS WILLING TO TAKE.** Make it very clear and specific. (You'll know it's clear and specific if you are able to tell conclusively that he or she has either done it or not done it.) Suppose an architect says to you, "I'm speaking to the National Association of Commercial Architects in two weeks." You might ask if she is comfortable calling clients, dormant clients, or people she's always wanted to meet and inviting them to the talk. She might also ask their opinions of what they'd most like to hear on the topic. If she likes the idea, she might say, "Sure, I'll call one of my clients." That's not good enough. Why? No names and no time frames have been given. You might ask if there are any clients or dormant clients she can think of inviting. If the answer is no, help her think of at least one name. Frequently, a name will pop into her head. Ask for the name and proceed to the next step.

2. **GET A TIME-DATED COMMITMENT TO TAKE THAT ACTION.** Without a date by which someone agrees to do something, you are not having a conversation for action. In my previous example, you might ask the speaker if she has given thought to when she might call this client and invite him to the talk. I prefer to let the professional choose the date rather than dictate when to take action. It gives the person control, a huge need for most people. Suppose she says, "I'll call in a week or two." Keep pressing for a date until she gives you one.

3. **IMMEDIATELY ASSESS THE PROBABILITY OF IT HAPPENING.** It's critical to read the body language of the professional who makes the commitment. It may give you clues as to his comfort level with the action he's committed to taking. The smaller the step you ask someone to take, the higher the probability that the person will do it. For example, the probability of me starting a year-long daily exercise program is vastly different from me going running once in the next three days. There are several factors that will reduce the probability of the professional taking action. If the person you're coaching doesn't write down what he is committing to, your odds almost immediately fall below 50 percent. It also depends on the length of time it will take to carry out a commitment. Imag-

ine getting a busy professional to read this entire book, versus reading Chapter 3.

4. INCREASE THE ODDS. Only agree to something that has above a 90 percent chance of happening. If the professional offers to do something you think has less than a 90 percent chance of happening, propose something with a higher probability. This is where the real added value of coaching comes into play.

Be ruthless about securing commitments that have a high probability of happening. Doing anything less will reinforce the professional's sense of inadequacy, quash a sense of momentum, and waste your time spent on following through.

5. WRITE IT DOWN IN YOUR CALENDAR IMMEDIATELY! Enlist a top-notch assistant to help you be more effective in follow-up. If you fail to follow up, I can nearly guarantee that the professional who has committed to action will not do what he or she says. Does this mean you'll have to remind the person for the rest of eternity? No. Only until a realization that you take every commitment seriously. If you consistently follow through, you will find that others become much better at following through because they know you won't forget. Some people will catch on after one or two of these episodes. Others may take much longer.

6. FOLLOW UP. Encourage the person you are coaching to call you and debrief. Or ask for permission to call him or her to debrief. Follow up when the due date arrives on the action step and ask how it went. Ask questions such as these:

- "How did your meeting go?"
- "How did your phone call go?"
- "What aspects of the meeting went well?"
- "In hindsight is there anything you might have done differently?"
- "Did anything happen that surprised you?"
- "Were you able to get an advance?"

- "What part of your meeting do you think he responded to best?"
- "Which questions do you think had the greatest impact?"

It may seem silly to have to keep after adults to do that which they agreed to do, but the reality is that most professionals would rather simply practice their trade. Your effectiveness as a firm leader and motivator will skyrocket if you have just three conversations for action each day and follow through on every one of them. Yes, this creates a corresponding obligation on your part to follow up three times, but how badly do you want to change the firm's culture and help it grow?

Most professionals are neither lazy nor unmotivated about marketing; they are fearful.

$$\boxed{44}$$

HOW COACHING CAN CONTRIBUTE TO YOUR SUCCESS

HOW IS COACHING DIFFERENT FROM TRAINING?

Many people confuse training with coaching. They are not synonymous terms. *Training* usually occurs in classrooms, while *coaching* occurs before, during, and after actual meetings with your clients and prospective clients. Training is mass-produced learning. Coaching is hand-painted learning. Coaching is dramatically more effective in building skills than is training. In a study done by best-selling author Neil Rackham, he found that 87 percent of the skills taught to someone are lost in one month without effective coaching.[1] If that's true, then 87 cents of every training dollar are wasted without coaching.

Just because your professionals can regurgitate a definition learned in a workshop does not mean they will ever apply the concept in the real world. That's where coaching pays big dividends. For example, a consultant met with a prospective client and came back from the meeting excited. During the debriefing telephone call with me, she said, "I got an advance!

The client wants me to meet with his president!" ("Advance" is a term discussed in an earlier chapter.) My reply was, "Great! When is it?" At that moment, she realized there was no specific date on which the client agreed to meet, which means she hadn't obtained an advance yet. This conversation happened six days after the workshop. This professional learned the concept of an advance on the day of the workshop, but she didn't learn the skill until six days later. Without coaching, she may never have learned the skill. She also learned what she can do the next time this situation arises to be sure she doesn't let the same thing happen again. For this reason, I think of coaching as time-released learning.

Very few professionals seek out coaching assistance. Why? It never occurs to them or they see marginal value in it. They may even find it personally insulting to depend on someone else. Professional service providers are ferociously independent people. Yet the ones who receive coaching will learn far more and get better results than the professionals who don't. Our highest paid sports stars are poster children for the power of coaching. You never saw Michael Jordan reject Phil Jackson's coaching. To the contrary, great athletes are usually the most coachable people in sports.

There are dozens of ways an effective coach can help your marketing effort. Here are ten:

1. HELP YOU SELECT TARGET CLIENTS. Most professionals think too generally about their marketing. A coach can help you focus on capturing specific clients. Keep the size of the list workable. Targeting 20 clients is too many. Focus instead on two or three.

2. INCREASE CONFIDENCE DURING MEETINGS. A Toronto professional was very resistant about contacting someone whom he considered a prospective client. With the help of a coach, he developed and rehearsed the questions he might ask this person during a phone call. He also defined a concrete objective he intended to work toward during the call—namely, set a meeting. After considerable rehearsal, he

mustered up the courage to call, set a meeting, did homework before the meeting, and went into the meeting confident and relaxed. His contact did not give him any work directly, but she gave him a referral that did generate work.

3. POINT OUT THE LINK BETWEEN BEHAVIOR AND RESULTS. An outstanding coach shows people the link between their behavior and the results they are currently getting. They break the selling process into bite-sized pieces. Many professionals go into their first meeting hoping to get a file. That's way too ambitious in most cases and leads to rejection. At the other extreme, professionals go into meetings with no objectives whatsoever. In those cases, they walk away empty-handed. One of the most powerful lessons learned by my clients is that lack of preparation (behavior) leads to rejection (result).

4. THINK OF ADVANCES BEFORE YOU HAVE A CLIENT MEETING. An advance is a specific next step that every professional ought to define as a possible outcome to marketing meetings. A coach can help you brainstorm several possible advances you might work toward during your meeting. Most professionals don't give any thought to the outcome they seek.

5. THINK OF OPTIONS. Devise creative ways to generate interest in your services and get in front of your target audience. One marketing director, prior to working with her current professional service firm, sold textiles. She had been trying to provide a sample to a building committee that had invited bids but would not let her participate. She finally got their attention by sending them a pizza box containing the sample via special delivery. She subsequently was granted a meeting—and the sale.

6. DEVELOP QUESTIONS TO ASK DURING A MEETING. A coach can help you develop penetrating questions that you can ask your contact. One professional had agreed to write out the questions he intended to ask his prospective client. Upon receiving this list, the coach could not find one question on the entire page. The coach urged this professional to rework his talking points into questions.

7. REVIEW AND ENHANCE YOUR MARKETING WORK PRODUCT. Coaches can review all of your marketing work product, not just your response to RFPs, and offer ideas on enhancing them. In one firm, the marketing director intercepted a letter that was to go out describing the firm's environmental services. The marketing director dramatically reworked the letter to flow more like a decision tree analysis. The client loved it. She contacted the professional and said, "Do what's in that letter." I suspect that the original version of the letter would have gone in the trash.

8. PREPARE FOR SPEAKING ENGAGEMENTS. Your coach can help you prepare for speaking engagements that dramatically increase your chances of generating meetings with your target or ideal clients. Whenever I hear of professionals who are scheduled to speak, I ask them how they intend to engage the audience in a dialogue. Most professionals have no clue how to do it. (See Chapter 34, "Using Speaking to Win New Clients.")

9. CONDUCT DEBRIEFINGS. Debrief after every marketing meeting or activity to help you learn from every experience. The most valuable lessons learned from everyday life can't always be found at the surface. Sometimes you have to dig. The number of learning experiences per meeting will be higher when you debrief. For example, contrast the uncoached professional who, at best, concludes after a meeting that he should have prepared better with the professional who, after coaching, concludes, "I should have searched the company website, pulled up all articles from Nexis, and made a note of just how fast they were growing and what markets they targeted for expansion."

10. SURMOUNT OBSTACLES. Everyone is going to hit what appear to be obstacles and dead ends during the relationship-building process. A coach can help you get past these moments. In one case, a professional I had been coaching wanted to target a specific client, but didn't know anyone within the target company. I was able to show him three different avenues for meeting people in the target company. One involved asking a former employee that the professional knew well to make an introduction; another involved inviting the CEO to speak to a group to which the professional belonged; and the final way was to attend a conference the company was likely to attend as an exhibitor.

Who should be your coach? Whoever is willing to do it. If your firm has marketing staff, befriend them before your next beauty contest or marketing meeting. Or you might seek out another professional in your firm as a sounding board. Afterward, you can also talk through how you think it went. If you're a solo practitioner, find another professional, say an accountant or architect, who will buddy up with you and is interested in building his or her practice. And give yourselves the right to hold each other accountable for doing what you say you're going to do. Coaching has a way of making serendipity happen.

Giving effective feedback is a motivational tool,
more powerful than money.

45

GIVING EFFECTIVE FEEDBACK

HOW DO I GIVE OTHERS IN MY FIRM FEEDBACK?

According to the November 2000 issue of *Fast Company* magazine, the single most important variable in employee productivity and loyalty was not pay, perks, benefits, or workplace environment, but the quality of the relationship between employees and their direct supervisors. What people want most from their supervisors is the same thing kids want from their parents: Someone who sets clear and consistent expectations, cares for them, values their unique qualities, and encourages and supports their growth and development.

Developing and encouraging people systematically is critically important to any firm, but professionals don't develop by accident. There is no better tool for developing people fast than giving feedback. Yet it is the rare professional who spends any time giving feedback.

I have been told by hundreds of professionals that the feedback I've given them is the first meaningful feedback they've received during their careers, which sometimes span decades. Developing people fast should be a differentiator, but I don't know of a single firm that even tries differentiating on that basis. I am certain there are hundreds of clients who would flock to professional service firms that excel at developing people. You can develop skills at least two or three times faster with effective feedback. Studies have shown that those who receive no feedback suffer the same kind of blow to their self-confidence as those who are criticized![1]

Failure to give feedback does untold damage to the human spirit. I have worked with many professionals who, in private, lavish praise on their associates but never share their comments directly with those associates. At the other extreme, giving brutal feedback can cover for pure aggression—an attack disguised as "helpfulness."[2] Here are some guidelines that you should follow whenever you are giving effective feedback:

LET THE PERSON RECEIVING THE FEEDBACK ASSESS HIS OR HER OWN PERFORMANCE

Most professionals are very good advocates, but this is one area where your "strength" is definitely a weakness. Always ask your protege to assess himself and his performance first.[3] Often he will be harder on himself than you would have been and more inclined to change as a result. For example, if you observe a young associate taking a deposition, start by asking, "Charlie, how do you think the deposition went?" This gives your associate some control over the learning process, which is an important psychological need. Doing this also provides great insight about his thinking and motivation.

START WITH THE POSITIVES

Always begin giving feedback by stating what you like about your associate's performance. Put a lot of energy into finding the positives, not just one perfunctory compliment. Articulate six or seven things about her performance that you liked. If you start with what needs improvement, she won't hear the positives and you won't reinforce the effective behaviors she is already exhibiting. This one is hard for professional advisors because we are trained to look for the downside.

Be Specific

Find current examples of the behavior that you like or that you want to change. Instead of saying, "You weren't listening," say "Your failure to let him finish his sentences left him with the impression you weren't listening." Instead of saying, "You were 'confrontational' with the client," say "Do you realize the effect you had on the client when you commanded him to 'look at me, Mr. Atkins'?"

Focus On One or Two Key Behaviors; Don't Overload the Person

No human being can work on 20 things at a time. Limit areas for improvement to one or two key behaviors that will really make a difference in performance.[4] If a professional has a bad habit of cracking knuckles during client meetings and is a poor listener, have her work on her listening skills and worry about the knuckles later.

Provide the Feedback in One-on-One Closed-Door Sessions

Don't give feedback in practice group meetings or where others can overhear. If and only if you want to become a member of the "morale suppression team" should you berate someone in front of peers or co-workers. Interacting one-on-one is an awesome way to build the relationship.

Be Very Timely with the Feedback

You can't give feedback once every three months and have it be effective. Try giving the feedback, both positive and negative, as soon after the behavior is observed as possible. Waiting two weeks to give the feedback is almost the same as not giving feedback at all. Don't let the sun set without giving it. If you wait and only give feedback when someone's performance has slipped drastically, you are wasting a precious resource: time. Sporadic feedback will delay skills development. You don't have to spend more time giving feedback than you do brushing your teeth.

Following these guidelines won't mean much unless you genuinely care about the person to whom you're providing the feedback. These techniques, when combined with a genuine caring attitude, can radically transform almost anyone's performance.

Providing meaningful feedback is a lightning fast way to transfer knowledge from one professional to another. If you say, "I don't have the time," what you're really saying is "This isn't a priority." Make the giving of feedback a daily priority starting now. Try it with someone today. Your professionals will develop at warp speed, and your clients will really appreciate it.

Coaches can't make fear go away, but they can help people act in spite of their fear.

46

INCREASE YOUR CREDIBILITY THROUGH COACHING

HOW WILL COACHING INCREASE MY CREDIBILITY?

One of the fastest means of earning respect in professional firms is to help professionals achieve success. In my work with professional service firm leaders throughout the world, I've noticed the ones who command the most respect tend to be very good at coaching. I've been known to ask marketing partners and directors this question: "How many professionals in your firm won't make a move in the marketing arena without you?" The number they throw out is usually correlated to the amount of their compensation. If only one or two seek your counsel before marketing meetings, you're likely to be making less than six figures. If dozens seek you out for help with marketing meetings, you'll earn a six figure salary in no time.

Every day you will be presented with opportunities for enhancing your credibility, whether you run the firm, you're a section leader, or a professional in a two-man firm. Here are several skills you should hone to raise your credibility.

Have More "Conversations for Action"

(See Chapter 43,"Jump Starting Others' Marketing Efforts")
The best thing you can do to increase your effectiveness is to make every conversation you have with a professional a "conversation for action." What that means is you never let the professional you are coaching walk away from a meeting without specific time commitments to take action. Being good at this skill will place added demand on your follow-up skills. The more conversations for action you stimulate, the more follow-up you will need to do. Your professionals will, however, achieve far more success. It's a virtuous cycle.

Give Frequent Feedback

There are six steps to giving effective feedback: (1) To start, let the person assess his or her own performance; (2) When you begin, start with the positives; (3) Be specific; (4) Focus on one or two key behaviors—don't overload the person; (5) Provide the feedback in one-on-one closed-door sessions; and (6) Be very timely with the feedback.

Never withhold valuable feedback. The marketing director at one large firm failed to pass along candid and painful feedback she received from a prospective client after a beauty contest with a professional in her firm. This professional found out about it three years later and was apoplectic. He felt as if he had been denied the chance to work on his shortcomings for that three-year period. He tried mightily to get her fired. He didn't succeed, but that marketing director learned a priceless lesson: Never withhold feedback, even when it might be painful for you to deliver it.

Look for Teachable Moments

Any great coach is always on the alert for the teachable moment. A teachable moment happens when the professional you are coaching pauses to reflect on a recent meeting or experience for the purpose of learning from it. This can become a daily event if you're vigilant. One frequent lesson learned by many professionals is to talk less and listen more during marketing meetings. I find many people making the same mistakes repeatedly without a coach.

LESSONS LEARNED FROM COACHING'S FRONT LINES

Some of you probably feel as if your credibility is on the line every day. I've coached thousands of professionals who have widely varying abilities for, and commitment to, the process of relationship building. Those experiences have taught me some valuable lessons about what increases and what detracts from my credibility. Some of those lessons are as follows:

1. HELP YOUR TEAM MEMBERS PREPARE FOR MARKETING MEETINGS. No decent coach ever lets players go into a game without specific strategies for "winning," and neither should you. Great coaches go further: They prepare their players for overcoming obstacles they'll likely encounter during the game.

2. GIVE THEM A WAY TO KEEP SCORE. You would be amazed at the number of professionals who believe they should try to get paid work from every marketing meeting. That is a recipe for rejection. Instead, take the pressure off by teaching your team how to get to the next step. If your professional has a meeting with Alice, suggest he attempt to secure another meeting or a conference call with Alice. That's much easier than trying to "get work" from Alice.

3. BECOME GOOD AT PREDICTING THE FUTURE. This isn't as hard as it sounds. Two recurring situations illustrate this. First, if your professionals don't prepare before heading off to marketing meetings, you can bet they will experience a much higher level of rejection. Forewarn them when you feel they are headed for trouble. Second, if your professionals don't write marketing actions into their calendars, most will forget their commitments to take action.

4. FOCUS ON WHAT THE PROFESSIONAL NEEDS TO LEARN. The tendency when coaching is for the coach to gravitate toward things he or she knows, rather than focus on what the professional wants to learn. When you as the coach know how to do what the professional wants to learn, you will gain credibility. If not, you'll lose credibility fast. For example, if a professional wants to learn how to ask for referrals and the coach doesn't know how it's done, he or she won't be of much help and credibility will suffer.

One professional had a client named Ron who was sponsoring a breakfast with a group of community leaders. This professional was invited to the breakfast and asked his coach for ideas on how to approach it. His coach suggested he call Ron ahead of time to find out who would be attending and ask if there were anyone in particular he ought to make a point of meeting during the breakfast. The professional loved the idea and executed it to perfection. In this case, credibility was gained. It could have been lost if his coach had had no clue about what he should do.

5. FIND A HUMOROUS WAY TO HOLD PEOPLE ACCOUNTABLE. When professionals fail to return three of my phone messages, I leave a message that says they are in "Maraia's Marketing Doghouse" and the only way to extract themselves from it is to return my call. This usually prompts a return call. If it doesn't, I sometimes leave another message saying, "I have left instructions in my will for my children to continue to follow up with you to find out how your meeting went." ☺

6. HOLD THEM ACCOUNTABLE TO THEMSELVES. Coaches help people keep promises they make to THEMSELVES! Many professionals have great intentions, but they fail to activate them. One professional said her conversations with her coach were the kinds of conversations she should have with herself but never does.

7. TIME YOUR FOLLOW-UP CALLS OR VISITS AROUND THEIR ACTION STEPS. Don't wait until the practice group or marketing committee meeting to follow up. Your follow-up call or visit to their office should be the same day as the event for which you're coaching. This will communicate volumes about your interest in them.

Boundless opportunities to increase your credibility arise every day. If you apply the ideas set forth above, you will win over even the most hardened cynics. If you're a leader within a firm and you want to create a high performance organization, follow these simple guidelines and watch your credibility skyrocket.

PUTTING THIS
BOOK TO WORK

Don't use planning as a delay tactic for getting face-to-face with clients and prospective clients.

47

ANNUAL PLANNING GUIDE FOR PROFESSIONALS

WHAT ARE THE ELEMENTS OF A PERSONAL MARKETING PLAN?

We all know that people who set goals vastly outperform those who don't. Yet, most people don't set goals. Have you written down your goals for the current year? If you need a quick tool for doing so and aren't sure where to begin, use the following to give you a quick start on planning. It should take one hour or less to complete.

Anyone who has set and achieved goals knows the rush from doing so. If filling in all these blanks is too much, then fill in the first three lines and do nothing else until you've completed them. Most business professionals would have a banner year if they actually captured three new clients for the entire year.

A 60-Minute Planning Guide for Professionals

1. I will complete this form within _____ days.

2. My three primary target clients for this year are
   _____, _____,
   and _____.

3. I will meet with [prospective client/existing client] by
   _____ for the purpose of _____.

4. I will do research on [prospective client/existing client]
   by _____.

5. The needs of this person are _____,
   _____, and _____.

6. I will ask the following questions of this person during
   my meeting:
   _____?
   _____?

7. The advances I will work toward during phone calls or
   meetings are _____.

8. I will ask _____, my primary contact at client
   _____, to introduce me to two new people
   who work for that same client. (This is designed to
   expand your contacts with an existing client.)

9. I will reduce my reliance on client _____
   from ___ percent of my revenues down to ___ percent.

10. I will conduct ___ client satisfaction interviews with
    my clients this year. I will start with clients
    _____ and _____
    in the first quarter; _____ and
    _____ in the second quarter. I will
    do these in person.

11. I will meet with ___ prospective clients this quarter.

These are people I know for whom I'm not doing any business.

12. I will devote ___ hours to marketing and business development each quarter of this year. I will diligently keep track of the time I invest in this area.

13. I will meet with ___ people in my network each quarter of this year. I will start by meeting with

_____, _____, and

_____.

14. I will meet with ___ of my partners each quarter of this year. I will start by meeting with _____ by February 1, _____ by February 15, and _____ by March 1, etc.

15. I will meet or speak with ___ referral sources each quarter of this year. I will start by calling _____ by January 30. The list of questions I will ask are

_____?

_____?

16. I hope to generate ___ unprompted referrals during each quarter of this year.

17. I will write ___ articles this year and place them in publications that my clients read. My target publications are _____ and

_____.

18. I will speak ___ times during the year at industry or trade conferences where my prospective clients congregate. (Related questions: Where am I currently scheduled to speak and on what dates? How do I get on the agenda for those conferences? Do I know the name of the chair of the speakers' committee? If not, can one of my clients or partners make an introduction or sponsor me as a speaker?)

19. I will learn ___ new skills this year that will increase

my value to the market. (For instance, I will learn about capital funding in the biotech field to better serve the needs of my environmental clients. I will learn how to use the Internet or Lotus Notes or Power-Point so I can better communicate with my clients and/or my partners in other states or countries.)

20. I will call dormant clients _____
and _____ by _____ to
ask them if they would like to receive the firm newsletter or ask them to join a group I belong to or speak to a group I belong to.

(If you would like a downloadable electronic version of the Annual Planning Guide, visit my website at www.mark-maraia.com.)

Go light on planning and heavy on execution.

48

THE MARAIA MARKETING CHALLENGE

At the end of my workshops I issue "the Maraia Marketing Challenge," so it's only fitting that I do the same thing at the end of this book. I ask each participant to take one marketing action per day for the next month. Some automatically assume that this will involve too much time. When you break it down, however, you realize it's workable and not all that time-intensive. The universe of people you might call includes clients, prospective clients, dormant clients, friends, referral sources, firm alumni, and college or grad school alumni, to name a few. In a typical calendar month, there are between 20 and 22 business days, but meeting the challenge does not require you to contact 22 different people.

To keep track of this, you might keep a journal of all your marketing activity for the month. What follows is a fictitious example (including fictitious names) of what your marketing journal might look like after it's completed. After each entry, I have listed in parentheses the amount of time taken for each activity. The journal of a rainmaker will include many more contacts each month than the professional who is sales-phobic. The one set forth below is somewhere in between.

Wednesday, January 2: Called prospective client Fred Maxwell @ Dunsun Corp. Left a message. (1 min)

Thursday, January 3: Called Fred Maxwell @ Dunsun Corp. Left no message. (1 min)

Friday, January 4: Called prospective client Betsy Boushell, in-house counsel at Revere, Inc. Left message. (1 min)

Called alumni of firm who went in-house at BHAG Corp. Left message. (1 min)

Monday, January 7: Called friend from college who is now at GE and caught up on life. (15 min)

Tuesday, January 8: Called Charlie Tyler, my best referral source, and arranged lunch on January 21. (2 min)

Wednesday, January 9: Called Fred Maxwell @ Dunsun Corp. Left no message. (1 min)

Thursday, January 10: Attended law school alumni meeting. Made contact with three friends, two of whom are in private practice and one of whom is now in-house. (90 min)

Friday, January 11: Stopped by partner Alex Martin's office and set lunch for January 17 to discuss cross-selling opportunities. (5 min)

Monday, January 14: Called Fred Maxwell @ Dunsun Corp. Left message. (1 min)

Tuesday, January 15: Called Karen Munson to thank her for referral. (5 min)

Called prospective client Betsy Boushell, in-house counsel at Revere, Inc. Left message. (1 min)

Wednesday, January 16: Called favorite client Elliot Goldratt @ eWorks, Inc., and offered to tour their plant while I'm out visiting next week. Scheduled tour for January 23. (4 min)

Thursday, January 17: Lunch with partner Alex Martin. Asked two networking questions: "What exciting stuff are you working on these days?" and "How do I know when I'm talking to your ideal client?" (66 min)

Friday, January 18: Called dormant client Cliff Edwards at Derringer and closed the loop on advice given late last year to see how it turned out. (23 min)

Monday, January 21: Had lunch with Charlie Tyler. Offered to introduce him to prospective client Bob Glasser. (94 min)

Made call to Bob Glasser after lunch regarding his interest in three-way meeting with Charlie Tyler. Left message. (1 min)

Tuesday, January 22: Called Bob Glasser and explored his interest in three-way meeting with Charlie Tyler. He is interested. (11 min).

Sent e-mail to Charlie Tyler suggesting three possible dates for a three-way lunch. (4 min)

Wednesday, January 23: Took tour of favorite client eWorks, Inc., plant. (128 min)

Thursday, January 24: Called Fred Maxwell and set meeting for February 1. (5 min)

Friday, January 25: Called dormant client Anita Smith at Angel Investors. Left message. (1 min)

Monday, January 28: Called prospective client Betsy Boushell, in-house counsel at Revere, Inc. Left message. (1 min)

Tuesday, January 29: Called client Nate Latham to set meeting to gather client's feedback on Dumster acquisition. Left no message. (1 min)

Wednesday, January 30: Called client Nate Latham and set meeting on February 15 re: feedback on Dumster acquisition. (5 min)

Thursday, January 31: Called five people, three clients and two prospective clients, and invited them to my presentation in NYC at the Mega Conference on Feb. 28. (35 min)

The total amount of time devoted to all these activities is 8.38 hours. The breakdown on how this lawyer invested his marketing time is as follows: existing clients, 159 minutes; prospective clients, 38 minutes; dormant clients, 24 minutes; current referral sources, including his partners, 176 minutes; and people in his network, 106 minutes. Now I ask you? Is this kind of schedule realistic? A fair number of professionals wouldn't even consider many of these activities marketing, but things they would do anyway.

AFTERWORD

Rainmaking Made Simple emerged from my intense desire to share what I know about professional services marketing. I operate from the belief that the more meaningful connections you make with others, the more it feeds your soul. I want this to be the definitive "how to" book on the subject. I have not withheld any ideas in hopes you'll hire me for the "really great stuff." I have found that giving all I've got is the only way to operate a business, and the sames goes for writing a book. Of course, my knowledge base is constantly expanding because of my work, and it's a never-ending cycle. As my knowledge expands, I will update this book as warranted. (Meanwhile, visit my website at www.markmaraia.com for the latest news and strategies.)

Many of the ideas set forth in this book were first introduced through a monthly electronic newsletter that is distributed to more than 2,800 professionals in 25 countries. If you would like to receive this newsletter, go to www.markmaraia.com and click on the button that says Free Newsletter.

I would be delighted to hear from you about ideas for future editions. I love it when readers share their success stories with me. Tell me which chapters you found particularly helpful, and give me feedback on how you put these ideas into action. I'm particularly interested in knowing whether or not you accepted the Maraia Marketing Challenge in Chapter 48.

I welcome your suggestions for improvement. Please send them to:

Mark M. Maraia

e-mail: markmaraia@ earthlink.net

website: http://www.markmaraia.com

phone: 303-791-1042

fax: 303-791-1071

APPENDICES TO CHAPTER 17

Appendix A

You should consider one or more of the following sources when trying to learn more about a company:

1. Research reports done by all the major brokerage houses on the target client. This might include a conversation with securities analysts.

2. Value Line reports that tell you about an industry.

3. Standard and Poor's Directory and/or Dun & Bradstreet.

4. Other people whom you know in the field. For example, if you're a real estate lawyer, you should check with your contacts at the title company, leasing company, and even the building security company hired by the various buildings around town.

5. Non-decision makers you might know within the target company.

6. Check with your peers and support staff within your firm to see whether they have any relationships with people in the target company. If you know that one professional knows an industry very well, buy him lunch and have him give you an overview.

7. The website of the U.S. Department of Commerce, www.doc.gov.

8. Industry and trade magazines.

9. The local Chamber of Commerce.

10. Attend trade association meetings, preferably as a guest of your client, or go to the executive director of the trade associations to which the target client belongs.

11. Go to the company website of the target company. A company website will frequently give you executives' biographies, latest developments, and internal organization information not available elsewhere.

12. Go to the website of smaller companies that compete against the target client.

13. Call the marketing department of the target company and befriend someone.

14. Go to sellers of non-competitive products and services who sell to the targeted company.

15. Check the annual reports, 10Ks, and 10Qs of the target company.

16. Pull all articles from Lexis/Nexis or Westlaw/Dialog on the target company.

17. Read books about the company or industry, for example, Bill Gates' *The Road Ahead* or Andy Grove's *Only the Paranoid Survive*.

18. Check to see what your marketing director, librarian, and marketing department knows about an industry or company.

19. Get a briefing book on the company from *The Wall Street Journal* website ($49/year to use), www.wsj.com. It's an interactive service that has stock and investor reports, company and financial background, press releases, news stories, and usually a link to the company's website.

20. Another thing you can do to augment your internal library's marketing research capabilities is to hire a service company called Find/SVP based in New York City.

For a fixed monthly retainer (which begins at a steep discount to actual usage but will, with time, increase to more accurately reflect your actual usage) you can call in a company name and get well-screened and well-prepared articles, profiles, brokerage reports, trade news, etc. delivered back to you in two or three days. Find/SVP's phone number is 212-645-4500. The website is www.findsvp.com.

21. There are many websites you might check as well:

www.fedworld.gov. This is the doorway to all (or almost all) federal agency web pages. There is a tremendous amount of information available now from the government and, happily, most of it is current and accurate!

www.sec.gov. For financial information on public companies, and some that are not public but still have SEC filing requirements (such as REITs), you can't beat it.

www.ipocentral.com is a site with complete information about IPOs.

www.corptech.com has high tech company profiles.

www.wsrn.com is Wall Street Research Net.

www.hoovers.com provides business and company information from Hoovers, Inc.

www.dbisna.com/dbis/product/secure.htm. Dun & Bradstreet online. Searching is free; reports cost $20.

www.prnewswire.com/cnoc.html. Company News on Call: a searchable database of full-text company news releases.

www.amex.com.80/stocks/stklst1.html. The American Stock Exchange Company List: company headlines, stories/information.

www.hnt.com/bizwire/wire.htm. Business Wire: press releases concerning subscriber companies.

www.corpfinet.com. Corporate Finance Network: financial entity information resource/links to company home pages.

If you're trying to find out more about an individual, use a good Internet search engine such as Google.com, Yahoo.com, or Vivisimo.com to locate publications, websites, news articles, and the like.

The first-time gathering of information is very expensive, but over time your ability to get up-to-speed gets easier and faster.

Appendix B: NQA Worksheet

What preparation can I do before my meeting with [prospect's name]? (e.g., do an Internet search on the prospect's website; check court docket sheets, etc.)

1. NEEDS. What are the personal needs and fears of this person (e.g., control, power, feeling understood, saving time, industry knowledge, looking good to the boss, having fun, earning respect, etc.)?

2. QUESTIONS. What questions can I ask this person (e.g., What do you like about the firms you currently work with? Is there anything you would like them to do differently?)?

3. ADVANCES. (e.g., another meeting, a phone call, a meeting with a contact or someone else in his or her company, a meeting with this person and your partner.)

END NOTES

CHAPTER 1

1. Richard Bach, *Illusions: Adventures of a Reluctant Messiah*. New York: Dell, 1977.

CHAPTER 2

1. Albert Mehrabian, *Silent Messages*. Belmont, CA: Wadsworth, 1981.

CHAPTER 6

1. Rolodex is a registered trademark of Rubbermaid Corporation.

CHAPTER 7

1. Stephen Covey, *The Seven Habits of Highly Effective People*. New York: Simon & Schuster, 1989.

CHAPTER 20

1. *eCompany Magazine*, June 2000.

CHAPTER 21

1. Panel counsel is a list of our approved service providers.

CHAPTER 27

1. Author's conversation with Debra Snider, former executive vice president, general counsel, and chief administrative officer of Heller Financial. November 7, 2000.

CHAPTER 34

1. Neil Rackham, *SPIN Selling*. New York: McGraw-Hill, 1996.

2. ibid.

CHAPTER 39

1. Bill Cates (www.referralcoach.com), *The Referral Minute*.

CHAPTER 42

1. David H. Maister, *Managing the Professional Service Firm*. New York: The Free Press, 1993.

2. Stephen Covey, *The Seven Habits of Highly Effective People*. New York: Simon & Schuster, 1989.

3. Linda Richardson, *Sales Coaching: Making the Great Leap from Sales Manager to Sales Coach*. New York: McGraw-Hill, 1996.

CHAPTER 44

1. Neil Rackham, *Managing Major Sales*. New York: HarperBusiness, 1991.

CHAPTER 45

1. Daniel Goleman, *Working with Emotional Intelligence*. New York: Bantam Books, 1998.

2. Ibid.

3. Linda Richardson, *Sales Coaching: Making the Great Leap from Sales Manager to Sales Coach*. New York: McGraw-Hill, 1996.

4. Neil Rackham, *Managing Major Sales*. New York: HarperBusiness, 1991.

SUGGESTED READING
AND RESOURCES

Here is a list of excellent books and publications that are well worth your time to read. I recommend them highly. They are listed by category in the next section.

The Fifth Discipline (Peter Senge)

Managing the Professional Service Firm (David Maister)

The Maraia Minutes newsletter (Mark Maraia)

The Path of Least Resistance for Managers (Robert Fritz)

Rainmaking (Ford Harding)

Sales Coaching (Linda Richardson)

Selling the Invisible (Harry Beckwith)

The Seven Habits of Highly Effective People (Stephen Covey)

SPIN Selling (Neil Rackham)

True Professionalism (David Maister)

The Trusted Advisor (David Maister et al.)

There are many books and articles in the areas of marketing, sales, business development, business leadership, personal growth, skills training, and coaching for the professional services provider. This listing gives those that resonate most with my own attitudes and beliefs.

CLIENT SERVICE

Albrecht, Karl. (1988). *At America's service: How corporations can revolutionize the way they treat their customers.* Homewood, IL: Dow Jones-Irwin.

Albrecht, Karl. (1992). *The only thing that matters: Bringing the power of the customer into the center of your business.* New York: HarperBusiness.

Albrecht, Karl. (2002). *Service America in the new economy.* New York: McGraw-Hill.

Berry, Leonard L. (1999). *Discovering the soul of service: The nine drivers of sustainable business success.* New York: The Free Press.

Blanchard, Kenneth H. (1993). *Raving fans: A revolutionary approach to customer service.* New York: William Morrow.

Bly, Robert W. (1993). *Keeping clients satisfied: Make your service business more successful and profitable.* Upper Saddle River, NJ: Prentice Hall.

Carlzon, Jan. (1987). *Moments of truth.* Cambridge, MA: Ballinger.

Carr, Clay. (1990). *Front-line customer service: 15 keys to customer satisfaction.* New York: John Wiley & Sons.

Cottle, David W. (1990). *Client-centered service: How to keep them coming back for more.* New York: John Wiley & Sons.

Davidow, William H. (1989). *Total customer service: The ultimate weapon.* New York: Harper & Row.

Goldzimer, Linda Silverman. (1989). *I'm first: Your customer's message to you.* New York: Rawson Associates.

Kaplan, Daniel I. (1994). *Service success! Lessons from a leader on how to turn around a service business.* New York: John Wiley & Sons.

Kausen, Robert. (1988). *Customer satisfaction guaranteed: A new approach to customer service, bedside manner and relationship ease.* Coffe Creek, CA: Life Education, Inc.

LeBoeuf, Michael. (1987). *How to win customers and keep them for life.* New York: G. Putnam's Sons.

Liswood, Laura A. (1990). *Serving them right: Innovative and powerful customer retention strategies.* New York: Harper & Row.

Peppers, Don. (1997). *Enterprise one to one: Tools for competing in the interactive age.* New York: Currency/Doubleday.

Peppers, Don. (1999). *The one to one manager: Real-world lessons in customer relationship management.* New York: Currency/Doubleday.

Whiteley, Richard C. (1991). *The customer-driven company: Moving from talk to action.* Reading, MA: Addison-Wesley.

COACHING

Dotlich, David L., & Cairo, Peter C. (1999). *Action coaching: How to leverage individual performance for company success*. San Francisco: Jossey-Bass.

Dennis, Gregory. (1993). *Mentoring*. Washington, DC: Office of Research.

Harding, Ford. (1998). *Creating rainmakers: The manager's guide to training professionals to attract new clients*. Holbrook, MA: Adams Media.

Hendricks, Gay. (1996). *The corporate mystic: A guidebook for visionaries with their feet on the ground*. New York: Bantam Books.

Landsberg, Max. (1997). *The tao of coaching: Boost your effectiveness at work by inspiring those around you*. New York: HarperCollins.

Leonard, Thomas J., & Larson, Byron. (1998). *The portable coach: 28 surefire strategies for business and personal success*. New York: Simon & Schuster.

McCall, Morgan W., Lombard, Michael M., & Morrison, Ann M. (1988). *The lessons of experience: How successful executives develop on the job*. New York: The Free Press.

Miller, James B., & Brown, Paul B. (1993). *The corporate coach*. New York: St. Martin's Press.

Murray, Margo (2001). *Beyond the myths and magic of mentoring: How to facilitate an effective mentoring process*. San Francisco: Jossey-Bass.

Rackham, Neil. (1991). *Managing major sales: Practical strategies for improving sales effectiveness*. New York: HarperBusiness.

Richardson, Linda. (1996). *Sales coaching: Making the great leap from sales manager to sales coach*. New York: McGraw-Hill.

Vaill, Peter B. (1996). *Learning as a way of being: Strategies for survival in a world of permanent white water*. San Francisco: Jossey-Bass.

Zemke, Ron. (1996). *Coaching knock your socks off service*. New York: AMACOM.

LEADERSHIP AND MANAGEMENT

Abramson, Mark A., & Lawrence, Paul A. [Eds.]. (2001). *Transforming organizations*. Lanham, MD: Rowman & Littlefield.

Ailes, Roger, & Kraushar, Jon. *You are the message: Secrets of the master communicators*. Homewood, IL: Dow Jones-Irwin.

Autry, James A. (1991). *Love and profit: The art of caring leadership*. New York: William Morrow.

Barker, Joel Arthur. (1992). *Future edge: Discovering the new paradigms of success*.

New York: William Morrow.

Biech, Elaine. (1998). *The business of consulting: The basics and beyond.* San Francisco: Jossey-Bass/Pfeiffer.

Blanchard, Kenneth H., Zigarmi, Patricia, & Zigarmi, Drea. (1985). *Leadership and the one minute manager: Increasing effectiveness through situational leadership.* New York: William Morrow.

Block, Peter. (1993). *Stewardship: Choosing service over self-interest.* San Francisco: Berrett-Koehler.

Bracey, Hyler, et al. (1993). *Managing from the heart.* New York: Dell.

Byham, William C. (1998). *Zapp! The lightning of empowerment: How to improve productivity, quality, and employee satisfaction.* New York: Ballantine.

Carnegie, Dale. (1936). *How to win friends and influence people.* New York: Simon & Schuster.

Cohen, Allan R. (1990). *Influence without authority.* New York: John Wiley & Sons.

Collins, James C. (2001). *Good to great: Why some companies make the leap—and others don't.* New York: HarperBusiness.

Conner, Daryl. (1993). *Managing at the speed of change: How resilient managers succeed and prosper where others fail.* New York: Villard Books.

Cooper, Robert K. (1997). *Executive EQ: Emotional intelligence in leadership and organizations.* New York: Grosset/Putnam.

Covey, Stephen R. (1989). *The 7 habits of highly effective people* [sound recording]. New York: Simon & Schuster Sound Ideas.

Covey, Stephen R. (1991). *Principle-centered leadership.* New York: Summit Books.

Covey, Stephen R. (1999). *Living the 7 habits: Stories of courage and inspiration.* New York: Simon & Schuster.

Covey, Stephen R., Merrill, Roger A., & Merrill, Rebecca R. (1994). *First things first: To live, to love, to learn, to leave a legacy.* New York: Simon & Schuster.

Cox, Danny. (1992). *Leadership when the heat's on.* New York: McGraw-Hill.

DePree, Max. (1993). *Leadership jazz.* New York: Dell Publishing.

Drucker, Peter F. (1995). *Managing in a time of great change.* New York: Truman Talley Books.

Dyer, Wayne W. (1995). *Your sacred self: Making the decision to be free.* New York: HarperCollins.

Frankl, Viktor Emil. (1963). *Man's search for meaning: An introduction to logotherapy.* Boston, MA: Beacon Press.

Fritz, Robert. (1989). *The path of least resistance: Learning to become the creative force in your life.* New York: Ballantine.

Fritz, Robert. (1993). *Creating.* New York: Ballantine.

Fritz, Robert. (1999). *The path of least resistance for managers: Designing organizations to succeed.* San Francisco: Berrett-Koehler.

Gardner, Howard. (1995). *Leading minds: An anatomy of leadership.* New York: Basic Books.

Goldberg, Philip. (1983). *The intuitive edge: Understanding and developing intuition.* Los Angeles: J.P. Tarcher.

Goleman, Daniel. (1995). *Emotional intelligence.* New York: Bantam Books.

Goleman, Daniel. (1998). *Working with emotional intelligence.* New York: Bantam Books.

Goleman, Daniel. (2002). *Primal leadership: Realizing the power of emotional intelligence.* Boston, MA: Harvard Business School Press.

Hamel, Gary. (1996). *Competing for the future.* Boston, MA: Harvard Business School Press.

Hampden-Turner, Charles. (1990). *Charting the corporate mind: Graphic solutions to business conflicts.* New York: The Free Press.

Handy, Charles B. (1995). *Beyond certainty: The changing worlds of organisations.* London: Hutchinson.

Hawley, John A. (1993). *Reawakening the spirit in work: The power of dharmic management.* San Francisco: Berrett-Koehler.

Jaworski, Joseph. (1998). *Synchronicity: The inner path of leadership.* San Francisco: Berrett-Koehler.

Jeffers, Susan. (1992). *Feel the fear and do it anyway.* New York: Fawcett.

Johnson, H. Thomas. (1992). *Relevance regained: From top-down control to bottom-up empowerment.* New York: The Free Press.

Jones, Laurie Beth. (1995). *Jesus, CEO: Using ancient wisdom for visionary leadership.* New York: Hyperion.

Kriegel, Robert J., & Patler, Louis. (1991). *If it ain't broke—break it!: And other unconventional wisdom for a changing business world.* New York: Warner Books.

Lee, Blaine. (1997). *The power principle: Influence with honor.* New York: Simon & Schuster.

Lundin, William. (1993). *The healing manager: How to build quality relationships and productive cultures at work.* San Francisco: Berrett-Koehler.

Maister, David H. (1993). *Managing the professional service firm.* New York: The Free Press.

McCall, Morgan W. (1988). *The lessons of experience: How successful executives develop on the job.* Lexington, MA: Lexington Books.

Morecroft, John D.W. (Ed.). (2000). *Modeling for learning organizations.* Portland, OR: Productivity Press.

Morris, Thomas V. (1994). *True success: A new philosophy of excellence.* New York: G.P. Putnam's Sons.

Oakley, Ed, & Krug, Doug. (1994). *Enlightened leadership: Getting to the heart of change.* New York: Simon & Schuster.

Parikh, Jagdish. (1991). *Managing your self: Management by detached involvement.* Cambridge, MA: B. Blackwell.

Peters, Thomas J. (1987). *Thriving on chaos: Handbook for a management revolution.* New York: Alfred Knopf.

Peters, Thomas J. (1994). *The pursuit of wow! Every person's guide to topsy-turvy times.* New York: Vintage Books.

Peters, Thomas J. (1994). *The Tom Peters seminar: Crazy times call for crazy organizations.* New York: Vintage Books.

Phillips, Donald T. (1992). *Lincoln on leadership: Executive strategies for tough times.* New York: Warner Books.

Pollard, C. William. (1996). *The soul of the firm.* New York: HarperBusiness.

Roskind, Robert. (1992). *In the spirit of business: A guide to resolving fears and creating miracles in your worklife.* Berkeley, CA: Celestial Arts.

Rowan, Roy. (1986). *The intuitive manager.* Boston, MA: Little, Brown.

Ryan, Kathleen, & Oestreich, Daniel K. (1998). *Driving fear out of the workplace: Creating the high-trust, high-performance organization.* San Francisco: Jossey-Bass.

Schwartz, Peter. (1991). *The art of the long view: The path to strategic insight for yourself and your company.* New York: Doubleday.

Senge, Peter M. (1990). *The fifth discipline: The art and practice of the learning organization.* New York: Doubleday/Currency.

Senge, Peter M., et al. (1994). *The fifth discipline fieldbook: Strategies and tools for building a learning organization.* New York: Doubleday/Currency.

Shea, Gordon F. (1983). *Creative negotiating.* Boston, MA: CBI Publishing Company.

Sinetar, Marsha. (1991). *Developing a 21st century mind.* New York: Villard Books.

Wall, Bob. (1992). *The visionary leader: From mission statement to a thriving organization, here's your blueprint for building an inspired, cohesive customer-oriented team.* Rocklin, CA: Prima Publishing.

Wheatley, Margaret J. (1999). *Leadership and the new science: Discovering order in a chaotic world* (rev.). San Francisco: Berrett-Koehler.

Whyte, David. (1994). *The heart aroused: Poetry and preservation of the soul in corporate America*. New York: Currency/Doubleday.

SELLING AND MARKETING

Alessandra, Anthony, et al. (1987). *Non-manipulative selling*. Upper Saddle River, NJ: Prentice Hall.

Beckwith, Harry. (1997). *Selling the invisible: A field guide to modern marketing*. New York: Warner Books.

Beckwith, Harry. (2000). *The invisible touch: The four keys to modern marketing*. New York: Warner Books.

Bellman, Geoffrey M. (1990). *The consultant's calling: Bringing who you are to what you do*. San Francisco: Jossey-Bass.

Berry, Leonard. (1991). *Marketing services: Competing through quality*. New York: The Free Press.

Bly, Robert W. (1991). *Selling your services: Proven strategies for getting them to hire you (or your firm)*. New York: Henry Holt.

Bly, Robert. (1993). *Keeping clients satisfied: Make your service business more successful and profitable*. Upper Saddle River, NJ: Prentice Hall.

Boyan, Lee. (1989). *Successful cold call selling*. New York: American Management Association.

Burg, Bob. (1994). *Endless referrals; Network your everyday contacts into sales*. New York: McGraw-Hill.

Cathcart, Jim. (1990). *Relationship selling: The key to getting and keeping customers*. New York: Perigee Books.

Cohen, William A. (1991). *How to make it big as a consultant*. New York: AMACOM.

Hanan, Mack. (1970). *Consultative selling*. New York: American Management Association.

Hanan, Mack. (1989). *Key account selling*. New York: AMACOM.

Harding, Ford. (1994). *Rainmaking: The professional's guide to attracting new clients*. Avon, MA: Adams Media Corporation.

Hawken, Paul. (1987). *Growing a business*. New York: Simon & Schuster.

Heiman, Stephen E. (1998). *The new strategic selling: The unique sales system proven successful by the world's best companies, revised and updated for the 21st century*. New York: Warner Books.

Levinson, Jay Conrad. (1989). *Guerrilla marketing attack: New strate-*

gies, tactics, and weapons for winning big profits for your small business. Boston, MA: Houghton-Mifflin.

Levinson, Jay Conrad. (1992). *Guerrilla selling: Unconventional weapons and tactics for increasing your sales*. Boston, MA: Houghton-Mifflin.

Levinson, Jay Conrad. (1993). *Guerrilla marketing: Secrets for making big profits from your small business*. Boston, MA: Houghton-Mifflin.

Levitt, Theodore. (1986). *The marketing imagination*. New York: The Free Press.

Mackay, Harvey. (1997). *Dig your well before you're thirsty: The only networking book you'll ever need*. New York: Currency/Doubleday.

Maister, David H., Green, Charles H., & Galford, Robert M. (2000). *The trusted advisor*. New York: The Free Press.

Miller, Robert B. (1987). *Conceptual selling: The revolutionary system for face-to-face selling used by America's best companies*. New York: Warner Books.

Peppers, Don, Rogers, Martha, & Dorf, Bob. (1999). *The one to one fieldbook: The complete toolkit for implementing a 1 to 1 marketing program*. New York: Currency/Doubleday.

Putman, Anthony O. (1990). *Marketing your services: A step-by-step guide for small businesses and professionals*. New York: John Wiley & Sons.

Rackham, Neil. (1988). *SPIN selling*. New York: McGraw-Hill.

Rackham, Neil. (1996). *Getting partnering right: How market leaders are creating long-term competitive advantage*. New York: McGraw-Hill.

Rapp, Stan. (1987). *MaxiMarketing: The new direction in advertising, promotion, and marketing strategy*. New York: McGraw-Hill.

Ries, Al, & Trout, Jack. (1993). *The 22 immutable laws of marketing: Violate them at your own risk*. New York: HarperBusiness.

Shifflett, Alan. (2000). *Major account sales strategies: Breaking the six-figure barrier in consultative selling*. Boca Raton, FL: St. Lucie Press.

Sonnenberg, Frank K. (1990). *Marketing to win: Strategies for building competitive advantage in service industries*. New York: HarperBusiness.

Wilson, Larry. (1994). *Stop selling, start partnering: The new thinking about finding and keeping customers*. Essex Junction, VT: Omneo.

INDEX

feedback, 45, 52, 59, 60, 62, 83, 84, 91, 130, 189, 194, 201, 203, 206, 207, 235, 241, 242, 255, 256, 257, 258, 260

"feel the fear and do it anyway," 26

fees, 44, 49, 56, 79, 113, 118

fees, increasing, 83

follow-up, 33, 54, 61, 65, 66, 67, 68, 74, 128, 175, 182, 190, 194, 196, 229, 247, 262

Forbes, 211

Fortune, 62, 211

fun, 15, 17, 35, 115

G

giveaways, 193

golf, 181, 219, 220, 223, 227

H

Heller Financial, 119, 156

hierarchy of contacts, 31, 32

hiring, 51, 113, 227, 234, 236

homework, 98, 152, 220

I

IBM, 46, 212

Inc., 211

incentives, 25

Infinity, 46

Internet, 211, 213, 217, 228

Internet year, 212

introductions, 124, 125

K

keeping in touch, 46

knowledge of business, 211

L

Law Firm Governance, 119

lead with the need, 197

letters, thank you, 52, 241

letters, written, 33

Lexus, 46

listening, 11, 12, 13, 91, 92, 115, 153, 226

lunch, random acts of, 97, 98, 101, 142

M

Mackay, Harvey, 140

Maister, David, 202

Maraia marketing challenge, 269

marketing journal, 269

marketing malpractice, 99

matchmaking, 136

meditating, 38

meetings, 19, 31, 34, 60, 77,